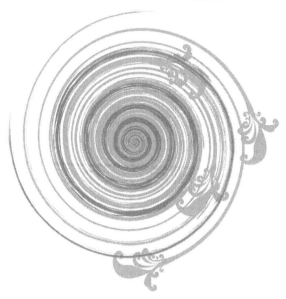

Love&mpasse

A look at 7 of the most challenging
transitions in spiritual development

Denise Richard

ISBN-13: 978-1468173031
ISBN-10: 1468173030

Cover design courtesy of Ezra Istiroti

Contents

7.... **Chapter 0** Beginnings: a personal story of awakening.

17.... **Chapter 1** The seed of awakening: those first impulses towards the possibility of self-realization.

35.... **Chapter 2** Reaching for understanding: questioning reality.

49.... **Chapter 3** The search for direct experience: looking for outside models that can support our spiritual path.

71.... **Chapter 4** The dark night of the senses: this great impasse is a confrontation with that with which we are not in alignment.

93.... **Chapter 5** The heartfelt revolution: the inner rebel that moves us deeper towards taking responsibility for the path we have chosen.

113... **Chapter 6** The dark night of the spirit: letting go of outside sources as a means to secure identity.

141... **Chapter 7** The invisible embrace and self-realization: integration of body, mind and spirit.

161... **Chapter 8** Security during a strong transition: the importance of community.

167... **Chapter 9** Tools for the Path.

187... **Notes**

189... **About the Author**

191... **Bibliography**

This book is intended as a means of understanding and support for those inclined towards self-realization. The spiritual path is not meant to be painful, but for some people it really is, for our process of devotion to God opens us to the deepest experience with Love and Grace. Therefore, please take this book as a potential guide for those passages in your life that may be difficult and all encompassing, not a blueprint that everyone will go through.

Chapter 0

Beginnings

THERE I WAS RIDING ON THE BACK OF A MOTORBIKE, clutching the waist of an elderly Hindu priest while whizzing through chaotic traffic in Varanasi, India. I was on my way to visit a Kali ashram, this particular one being a special place of refuge for those afflicted with leprosy. I could just imagine the snapshot: a middle aged western woman hanging on for dear life, no helmet, depending completely on the goodness of this long bearded Brahman. A man I had only met the previous day when he had given me an astrological reading of my present life transition.

We exited the stream of downtown traffic to enter a quieter area. The intensity of moving vehicles abruptly switched to a gentle country stride. We slowly puttered our way through side streets which were dirt roads no bigger than a one way lane. The local foot traffic was not only dense with people but also included chickens, goats, cows and donkeys pulling carts.

When we arrived there were two huge gates before me that glistened with fresh red paint. I got off the bike. It felt great to have my feet on the ground again as I watched people scurry around us.

There was nothing of familiarity around me. I had never been to India, never been in an ashram, and never been exposed to anyone with leprosy. I have to admit I was a little scared being so far out of my element. I didn't know what to expect, and though I was anxious my excitement outweighed my fear.

As I walked through the gates with this kind gentleman by my side I saw a small compound contained within a cinderblock wall. All along the periphery inside of this wall were small windowless huts that I think were made of mud. Each one was painted a different shade of blue and within the centre of all this was a huge black and red statue. It was a representation of the Hindu Goddess Kali, the wrathful mother whom Hindu's perceive to be the goddess of death. It is she who dissolves all illusion, egoistic traps and attachments. She had fierce, bulging eyes and a bright red tongue suggesting her wrathful determination to cut away our illusionary trappings and return us to a more harmonious order. I began to understand why she was the governess of this ashram. In her fiery intense persona she is a divine mother who offers a safe harbour for those suffering the ill effects of inertia in their life.

My present fears were somewhat eased as people with smiling faces approached me. Each received me with the traditional "namaste" greeting, placing their disfigured hands together at the heart. Some were on stretchers. All they could do was raise their arms in greeting. As they did so I saw the devastation of the disease that had afflicted them through their entire life. Their greetings and gestures touched me deeply. As I watched them gather slowly to encircle me, all kinds of feelings were churning inside. These people displayed a harmony within their circumstance I would not have expected. A sense of peace and tranquility was pervasive in their presence and their home...even the air smelt clean. I became aware how this environment clearly contrasted with what was going on inside me: a deep sense of emptiness and turmoil. They may have felt my own "dis-ease" for they led me to pray at the foot of the statue of Kali.

Through our prayers we asked the goddess to offer her strength and fierce love for the nourishment of all.

This little ceremony was done on a Saturday, Saturn's day, as suggested by my Brahman guide, to simultaneously invoke positive influences from the planet Saturn. As he explained it, I was born under Saturn which added a demanding influence in my life. Considered a masculine planet Saturn governs growth and movement. He brings definition to our lives through restriction, by slowing us down to face our deepest fears and limitations. More positively, Saturn also leads us towards deep worship, austerity and patience influencing matter over mind. He helps bring the intangible down to earth in restoration of that which is truly meaningful, eternally beautiful and divine.

Each in their own way, Saturn and Kali, have a polishing aspect that, though abrasive, appropriately wears away that which inhibits our unique expression of love. Like a good father or mother, both can bring heavy restrictions in order to provide the necessary ingredients to find real clarity of conviction and direction for the journey ahead.

Many times in my life I've experienced this kind of tough love. I've come to understand that cosmic and spiritual forces can ignite events that deeply rub away ignorance and naivete. The process is never pleasant, but in hindsight there is nothing more delightful than being awakened to new awareness and cultivating new seeds for wisdom and love.

Once our prayers were done the food cart that was my offering to the people was uncovered. The smell of freshly cooked rice, dahl, vegetables and Indian spices filled the air. As I looked into their eyes it registered in me how these people were completely dependent on the generosity of others. I felt honored and full of gratitude for the opportunity to share in this moment. I was handed a ladle and with joy proceeded to fill bowls until everyone had received their meal. Together we ate in silence.

I was greatly moved by the experience of this day. I loved how everything occurred without much to-do. I was absorbed into the flow of a culture that takes for granted spiritual process and heartfelt devotion. This journey to Varanasi marked a time of insight and exploration for me. It touched my longing and passion for understanding of how to cultivate deep spiritual care.

At this point in my life I had been consciously participating in a spiritual exploration for almost two decades. Yet, once again, I found myself feeling like a total beginner. I had learned and practiced many ways of developing awareness and had accumulated a wealth of information, context and experience from different eastern traditions. All this as well as my Catholic roots were being stirred up for reconsideration. Like a child's snow globe being shaken, I was being prepared for new configuration of perspective. I felt exposed and tender. I knew this feeling and recognized it as part of a familiar cycle. My discomfort signaled a time of transition.

It felt a little like cliff walking. It filled me with excitement yet demanded that I pay close attention to every step. These transitional times offer significant gateways for the development of awareness. We are given the opportunity to either resist or move towards greater consciousness. In choosing the path of consciousness we will inevitably be given the opportunity to meet the unknown and redesign our attitudes and perspectives towards life.

ON SPIRITUAL DEVELOPMENT

What is often unspoken is that our journey in spiritual development illuminates us at a cost. We seldom acknowledge that we are required to give something up in return for the gifts of awareness we receive. Nothing comes for free. The cost is usually what we are most unaware of, or attached to, that which falsely defines us and to which we feel intimately dependent. We confront a personal question along our spiritual journey: "In what act of bravery am I willing to engage in order to bring home the Holy Grail?"

When I began my journey, I did so with a strong belief that by being a spiritual person I would become a better one. This would make life easier, not just for me, but for everyone. If the development of our human nature was simple and straightforward, then this statement might be true; however, that is not exactly the case. Our growth is a complex journey through the deeply rooted mappings of the psyche, a truly messy and humbling walk. I see, in retrospect, that my arrogance and ignorance led me to believe that spiritual knowledge would prevent life from exerting itself upon me, and possibly save me from too much harshness.

This misguided belief is very common. Through the eyes of many who I have mentored, I have come to understand that this way of viewing things is the product of a naive and ill-informed culture. Too often there is little guidance of real understanding for personal needs and issues relating to individual spiritual growth and development.

For me, spiritual development is that ever growing movement towards kindness, empathy and equanimity. It is a way of developing awareness that refines our faculties and elicits consciousness of Heart. Ultimately the path of spiritual development has many forms and outward appearances. Regardless of what form is taken, the quality of heartfelt devotion, as I have experienced it, can lead us to individually claim the deeper essence of our being.

Each human being has the right to be held compassionately throughout their spiritual journey. Freely and safely choosing opportunities that will help reclaim a spiritual self-authority. This is an act of personal power that opens us to our full potential and is a great gift to humanity.

As I wrote earlier, the rub of Saturn's brillo-pad has brought much awareness to my spiritual journey. It has softened my crust and awakened enough courage in me to offer a compilation of stories and teachings that describe passages and processes we are inclined to go through during a long-term spiritual voyage.

In this book I document a journey through seven transitions. Each describes a process of development that is cyclical and moves us in spiraling fashion into further consciousness.

My inspiration emerged from personal experiences and a desire to bring more understanding to the intimate process of how challenging moments can inspire a richer spiritual life. It is my hope that the stories and examples chosen will cultivate clarity and activate personal growth. Although I use examples from a variety of spiritual traditions, I am not promoting any particular spiritual path. This book is about process. For simplicity's sake, the structure I present is written in a linear fashion, but in reality there is much overlapping and looping back and forth in the actual experience. May the following pages offer you support for a positive and fruitful journey.

I would like to acknowledge the many teachers, colleagues, friends who have supported me through these transitions. Each, in their own way, has helped shape my perspectives and inspired the creation of this book. In addition I would like to thank Carlos de

Leon who graciously shared his interpretation of the Seven Mansions as inspired by St-Theresa of Avila, and David MacMurray Smith for his deep love and technical support.

Chapter 1

The Seed of Awakening

IN OUR LIVES, SIGNIFICANT TRANSITIONS *may be preceded by a powerful sense of blocked movement or stagnation. This blocked state brings our attention to the limitations, belief systems, and characteristics that impede our spiritual growth. I refer to this condition as 'impasse' because it is as if there were a gridlock of opposing forces immobilizing and holding us in suspension. Even though it may feel*

stagnant, an impasse can inspire us to look in new directions and reconfigure our options.

The seed of awakening emerges from a moment of intuiting the possibility for self-realization. This first impasse can lead to a transition into a sense of possibility that somehow life can be experienced differently. At this time nothing is yet clearly articulated or contextually conscious, yet the energetic potential for the seed to grow is present. How the seed grows depends upon the quality of resonance it has within its environment. The process here is most often a slow and subtle shift in consciousness and is not necessarily outwardly displayed.

FIELD OF POTENTIAL

I love those little moments, Zen moments I call them, where for a very brief time everything stops. Everything is quiet. As if for a nano second I am sitting in the captain's chair of the Starship Enterprise - I'm offered a snapshot in the form of an overview of how intricate and interconnected things are.

Like the day I was walking across a busy intersection with my partner. We were on our way to the bank. As we arrived to the other side of the street, a very old woman approached, and literally put her face into my face and asked directly: "Do you want a job?" This was the moment we met Ena, a spirited woman who had been living in our neighbourhood for half a century. She was now over 100 years of age and wanted help with trimming her hedge.

Her strength of presence and clarity were unusual for someone her age. A lovely person with a delightful sense of humour, Ena had plenty to tell us of the life she had lived, the sadness's and loves she had been through.

This unusual moment put me in the captain's chair for one of those precious nano seconds. Enas' stories were describing smaller cycles within her larger lifecycle. She spoke of times that were, of things and people in her life that were now completed, yet she herself was continuing on. Her century of experience encompassed so many events, each one depicting its own lifecycle. Circles within circles and cycles within cycles metaphorically describing a vast interdependent complex of movement. She seemed intimately aware that she was immersed in the process of her own life completion. For a fleeting moment we were part of it. I felt a resonance with my own lifecycle and its relationship to that greater movement.

This scene was out of my daily context and once again I had been given a glimpse of the temporariness of things. Her hedge did get trimmed, and so did my attitude towards my day. Her gift was to slow me down, and gently settle me into considering passages I had gone through, moments that mysteriously changed my life.

One of the passages that came to mind was a time I was in the Andes with Puma, a Peruvian Elder whose

warm and sensible way could charm just about anyone. He was the designated medicine man and leader
for our trek up the Andean Salcantay trail into Machu
Picchu. I journeyed here as part of my continuing effort
to become acquainted with ancient places where people
had placed an energetic focus on a process of spiritual
development.

This majestic Salcantay Mountain is one of the highest peaks in the Peruvian Andes. For us to achieve this
ascent was the milestone signalling our near arrival into
the ancient archaeological site.

Here we were just before dawn. It was very dark and
still. I heard the tender sounds of a Peruvian flute. It
was Puma. My senses gently opened in preparation for
whatever was to come. An early morning chill brought
me to swaddle into my shawl as I took in the magic of
the moment. I saw the glow of the sun carving out the
edge of the mountain top in front of us. Soon the tips of
the entire range were ablaze with golden red rays flash-
ing through the darkness, illuminating Machu Picchu for
a new day. It was a stunning moment that imprinted
itself in my mind aesthetically, energetically and visu-
ally. Time slowed down. My awareness of my presence
on earth was magnified. Filled with gratitude, I felt an
intimate sense of grounded connection with existence.
The illumination of this ancient settlement encircled by
some of the highest peaks in the world has now for me
become a powerful symbol of that personal potential to

increase the quality of the resonance I could have with my environment.

Perhaps the most ancient symbol for wholeness is the circle. It has often been used in association with spiritual evolution. The circle is believed to hold something intrinsically divine and has been incorporated in spiritual symbols from many paths: the native American medicine wheel, the Buddhist Wheel of life, the Tao, the druids Stonehenge, the Christian's halo - to name a few. These circular symbols represent our intrinsic wholeness and completeness both personally and collectively.

Like the round shape of a sweet pie this symbolizes our hearts' desires for wholeness and contains what might feed the soul on its journey to attain self-realization. It's my experience that some people come to this life having already had their share of this pie. They exhibit unusual understanding, a sweet and loving consciousness, and an attitude of equanimity. In their presence there is a feeling that they may have perhaps digested a considerable portion of their pie, for their presence exudes a quiet wisdom.

As for the average person, learning to digest and integrate daily experiences, and benefit fully from the fruit of consciousness can be more than a full-time job. Life gives us a lot to feed on and it doesn't mean that it's all good for us. How we digest life's experiences becomes the question. How we relate to daily encounters will become the source for realizing our potential.

Relative to the seed of awakening, this implies the budding of the discerning self.

THE DISCERNING SELF

At this point the potential for growth begins to be more clearly sensed. This is an energetic activation of the dynamics in the relationship between our innate potential and what it needs for its realization. What is happening internally becomes a living potential edging its way towards our consciousness. In essence we have subtly achieved the activation of the blueprint upon which we can begin to distinguish self- awareness.

Life presents us with plenty of moments for this activation to take place, but due to the subtlety of this passage, it is easy to overlook it. The obvious is often difficult to see. As an example, a young client came to me for mentoring with concern of having no definition in his life. In his twenties he was feeling lost and daunted in face of his transition into adulthood. His family held no spiritual interests what so ever; yet, he himself was always curious about the world and all the spiritual "stuff," as he called it, that he heard of in discussions with friends. He was perplexed because he had longings for something more and sensed that this might be described as a spiritual life. This longing was strong enough to cause him to enquire and seek guidance.

He described his greatest challenge as that of being part of a social scene that made heavy use of drugs and alcohol. He found he was having trouble pulling away from this lifestyle to embark on a journey of his own. He was torn between the powerful influence of his peer group and his budding curiosity. He knew his public persona, the happy go lucky dude who enjoyed a lively night life, but didn't have a clue how to define himself outside of that...and the more he partied, the more he felt a deep pain well up inside.

He was at a crossroad that comes with these moments of impasse. The question of whether he would move forward into the unknown or remain in his present lifestyle would determine whether this impasse could be transformed into a transitional process. The seed for his awakening had been activated. He was now in dynamic relationship with his innate potential for self-awareness and what it demanded for its realization.

He knew he had to distance himself from his social scene, and listen to the promptings from his intuition. This was a very difficult process for him as it is for anyone in this circumstance. The twenties are a time for many when those mysterious and amorphous promptings begin to shake us into an awareness of our personal field of potential. The more we can find the courage to allow and facilitate these deep feelings, the more the blueprint for our self-awareness can evolve. This is the power of the first transition.

RESONANCE WITHIN OUR SURROUNDINGS

As the field for our potential growth comes into being what we first see are the foundations by which we presently define ourselves. These foundations are the imprints or primary experiences from our first years of life. Up to this point these primary experiences have guided us unconsciously. They influence how we move towards self-realization.

These imprints were modelled from our primary caregivers, usually Mom and Dad. During our first years, we see our significant caregivers as omnipotent beings. Our complete dependency on them and how our relationship plays out through these formative years will affect our process of awakening. It will influence what kind of path we choose and how we move through our transitional processes. This is because the imprints we model have a power in their familiarity. The known pattern is easiest for our perception to follow; it is the path of least resistance that continually repeats itself and dominates our way of seeing.

Until we become conscious of how strong these cycles of familiarity affect our perception, we will have very little influence on them.

The familiarity of daily routines and patterns desensitizes our awareness. By this I mean that when life is all mapped out and robotically practiced and predictable, our attentiveness dozes of into a comfy sleep like state. We sit back in a big arm chair and just let the days roll on. This state doesn't require much of us. We have little responsibility. We don't have to pay much attention. Awareness is not in practice and therefore remains limited. This becomes the framework through which we define ourselves until we find the means or circumstances to move beyond the familiar pattern and meet the unknown.

THE ROAD MOST TRAVELLED

There is an innate desire to uphold the familiar mappings until it becomes apparent that they serve us no longer. Our surroundings provide many options for maps to follow. Most cultures and communities have existing systems that are believed to support the soul on its spiritual journey. Our participation in these displays our willingness to take our place in helping to maintain the collective views, as is often expected of us. We are given general guidelines as to the nature of what is divine, how to relate with it and how to realize this in daily life. We learn what is spiritually acceptable and where the line is drawn according to rule.

A primary focus of most organized groups, especially religious groups, is to help secure the soul during its evolution and time on earth. At their entry level, these are not personalized training systems, they are not programs designed to necessarily adjust to meet the needs of the individual. Although I feel that the intention is to care for the individual, my experience is that the structures do more to support the masses for their general understanding of spiritual consciousness than provide an ability to respond to the unique evolutionary needs of the individual as they grow.

Whether the spiritual container we grew up with was given to us by our parents or one that we chose by design, it is often the case that at some point a shift will occur that will awaken a need for personal exploration. Opening to this shift invites us to accept the magnetism, repulsion, questioning and probing that our senses disclose as we discover our underlying needs; these are the promptings that set us on a more personal path. This process of investigation can inspire great change and give us the option to transform what feels stagnant into something really meaningful.

THE STORY OF MASTER CHEN

Many years ago I studied with an old Tai Chi master, Master Chen. He was the senior teacher or Grand Master of his lineage in Taiwan. A quiet and humble old man, he took great pride and dedication in meticulously sharing his knowledge. As is customary in the Taoist tradition, Master Chen invited our small group for an afternoon tea ceremony to mark his commitment to teaching us what he knew. What was implied and not spoken was that we were his students for life; he was now our one and only teacher. I came to understand this with time.

After about 5 years of training I came upon another Taoist healing form, that I was compelled to include in my learning. In pursuing this, my relationship with Master Chen began to feel strained. He didn't like that I was also studying with another teacher. For Master Chen, this was not acceptable. He could not share in my delight in the new form I was studying as he was fixed on how it was supposed to be, perhaps so that the teachings he gave were clearly preserved; it's hard to say. The strain of this unspoken tension created a rift between us. I was confused and very sad to see our relationship slowly dissolve. I had to go on my way and follow my path.

Now decades later, I more clearly understand the delicate balance between maintaining the boundaries of a formalised tradition and allowing for expansion beyond them. In my budding years with Master Chen I was opening to deeper spiritual matters through the seeds of my own awakening. This was an important stage of my spiritual walk and I was compelled to make space for it. The value of the tradition he set before me was the foundation that propelled me forward on my path.

Traditions are rich with the insights and the experiences of generations. They hold tremendous value. What I have found equally important is the maintenance of personal freedom within the patterns that traditions provide, so that they do not become another comfy chair that puts us to sleep.

TALKING ABOUT FREEDOM

A person can only grow in the context of their own seeking, their own questioning. Individual consciousness needs freedom in order to grow even in the framework of someone else's perspective. In strong group formats, individuals often depend on the validation and guidance of the leaders for evaluation of their spiritual evolution, and on the group energy to hold the circle of power intact. With great appreciation, we do need guidance, support, and protection on our individual paths and these voices of traditional authority are there for this purpose. Yet for consciousness to grow from within we must follow our own lead as well. The framework of any organization will only feel comforting and safe until that time when we meet the edge of our own self-reference within it, the edge of our own circle and begin to ask what is beyond this. These are often the rumblings for the seed of awakening.

MOVING BEYOND

To move beyond the perimeter of acquired knowledge we must be willing to embrace our impulses of desire and curiosity. In spiritual matters, our job is to follow these impulses using them as our compass. Our ability to be curious and continuously question is a crucial part of our spiritual process; it motivates our creative nature and invites a flexibility and openness of heart and mind. Curiosity goes hand in hand with excitement which brings forth a delight in discovery and supports us to learn new things and shed our limiting belief systems.

We are born with a marvellous ability to sense our surroundings and know how we feel about them. This innate skill is what allows us to become aware of our impulses and desires. In a way, each of us has been given our own compass and the opportunity to pioneer our way to self-realization. We see this naturally in the innocence of children as they describe the world from their own point of view. Children are open to asking their own questions and making up their own answers. They are free to create their own cosmologies and redesign them as necessary.

I remember a good friend telling me a story of when he was about 6 years old.

Little Bill was in Sunday school participating in a discussion about the wonder of what God must know - since God created the heavens and earth.

This was a topic that intrigued and provoked a lot of thought for him as he began to wonder what it would be like to know what God knows. In the week prior to the next Sunday school meeting he sat with this question until it suddenly occurred to him that he could know what God knows. He didn't know where this thought came from; it just popped into his head. It seemed reasonable that he could. It made sense to him.

The next week at Sunday school he was really excited to bring this up. When he did, he was told by the Sunday school teacher that nobody could really ever know what God knows.

This perplexed him. Though he didn't say so, for some reason he couldn't accept this answer. He sat with his reaction and with a feeling that he had said something wrong, but nothing was spoken of this.

Throughout the next week, little Bill pondered what his Sunday school teacher had said. This time a new notion came to his mind. He still felt that he could know what God knows. Yet, it also made sense to him that if he could learn something new, then God probably could too. So the next week at Sunday school, he stated that he still felt he could know what God knows but then he added; that by the time he knew what God knows now, God would probably have learned so much more that he would likely never catch up.

This was the way he found he could live within the paradigm of his own process and include the perimeters given by the world around him. This is a good description of the innocence within sensing and maintaining itself in our expanding universe.

It is awe inspiring that little Bill was so free to be empowered by his senses. He meets his world without concern for how his idea might fit within an existing structure.

This is one of the key qualities, a skill that will greatly assist in moving through an impasse. This first impasse arises when we are given the opportunity to re-acquaint ourselves with the power of our innocence. This need to rekindle will present itself throughout each impasse we face. The good news is that it is always there available to us, waiting for us to take to take advantage of the value it has.

As I mentioned at the beginning of the chapter, the power of this first transition is often a slow and subtle shift in consciousness and is not necessarily outwardly displayed. What our senses bring forward does not yet have any context that we can clearly understand. The ground we normally walk on begins to feel a little uneasy and unsure. At the same time we have this compelling sense to investigate. Nothing is defined. The following symptoms are indicators that an impasse may be imminent:

» The feeling that things are not quite right – "it's a gut feeling"
» The awareness that the social container feels restrictive in some way
» Questions are not being answered in satisfactory ways
» A calling and attraction emerge to look elsewhere
» A concern that investigating or looking outside might be bringing challenging consequences.

These points may seem simple enough; however; it is important not to dismiss them, for together they signal change that our spiritual life is opening up. When we wake up from our dozing state and begin to pay attention, we are likely to find ourselves meeting the edge of our own awareness. In spiritual matters this edge is presented in its first impulses through the signalling of an uneasiness that just won't go away. It's telling us that there is an option for a transition. For those who follow, these indicators will become familiar promptings that will recur through other passages for releasing stagnation and deepening awareness.

Human awareness has this mysterious quality, an inherent capacity for self- reflection. This is our deep purposeful engine that moves us towards fulfilling our unique way of being. Awareness is the substance that links the pieces of our personal puzzle together, giving our life a harmonious flow, that sense of oneness that so many people describe as a spiritual experience. Without awareness, there will be little spiritual growth and little capacity for change on any level.

I believe that impasses have predictable cycles that operate in a spiral fashion to bring us ever closer to our true nature. This first impasse reflects the awakening of the individual and refers to a budding of the discerning self as an entrance into our field of potential.

The power of familiarity mentioned before is part of what creates an impasse. When we fall out of awareness and become unconscious. If we also lose touch with our

innocent and inquisitive nature, we can become immobi-
lized. Alternatively in following the directives given innocently through our senses we may move into transition
and through the impasse into greater self-awareness.

Chapter 2

Reaching for Understanding

ONCE THE FIELD OF POTENTIAL IS ACTIVATED *the discerning self begins to question. These questions are driven by a thirst to more accurately identify ourselves and our relationship with our environment. Our activated senses trigger our intellect into action. The seeds of our awakening are now germinating into an intellectual pursuit to discover existing spiritual models that can satisfactorily provide a vehicle for their expression.*

The second impasse surfaces and signifies that we are now entering our spiritual infancy. We are innocently introduced to existential concerns. The nature of our existence is opened up for inquiry with simple yet profound questions: "Who am I? Why am I here? What is this life?" Like little Bill we identify with a need for distinctiveness in our understanding as well as a desire to fit in with our surroundings. The dynamic tension in this transition pulls between the desire to remain safely cocooned and the challenge to take on the responsibility that comes with following the drive sensed within. We experience our first movements towards self-identity as a spiritual being and our connection to it is by way of the intellect.

THE THIRSTY ENGINE

The intellect is distinct in its ability to coordinate the sensory information of our experiences into patterns and relationships with the outside world. It is commonly understood as an objective processer that organizes thoughts, feelings, and sensations into ideas and meanings. One of the intellect's purposes is to create a language to communicate with the world around us. The ability to create this language comes from within us; yet, at this stage, it is not articulate. Up to now our intellect has exercised itself through unconscious associations with the imprints modelled from our primary caregivers. Now we become intellectually active in seeking outside models to increase our field for association. The power of this intellectual search engine is considerable when combined with the thirst we feel to find frameworks within which to understand and identify ourselves.

This is not a singular event in our lives. There is no saying when it will first happen or whether it will happen again. Our first encounter with this kind of questioning may occur, and often typically does, when we are young adults. But this is not necessarily the case. For often this profound shift can occur later in midlife, at retirement, and very occasionally in childhood.

I recall meeting an elderly woman who described this process very well. She had just retired after 40 years of hard work and was looking forward to enjoying her last stage of life, free from the responsibilities of work and motherhood. Unexpectedly she discovered she was again entertaining questions she had asked herself when she was much younger.

Deep inside a new identity was forming and with it the old familiar questions were reaching for a new dimension of clarification. When those questions had arisen earlier in her life, she could answer them relatively easily: she was a mother caring for her children, or a nurse working with sick patients, she was a wife and a daughter. Now those categories no longer completely satisfied. Her yearning was different. She couldn't define it or talk about it very well. What she knew was that it had to do with something beyond her familiar world.

She was tongue tied. How could she describe that which she felt so clearly and deeply? What she was sensing reminded her of being a child gazing into the night sky, feeling that she had to pull herself back or she would be swept away by the vastness before her. She was drawn by the beauty and the majesty and at the same time scared of the immense unknown.

Although she couldn't put it into words, she was at the threshold of the second impasse. Her senses were in high gear and preparing her for action. The reality of her existence triggered a degree of personal inquiry, more powerful than she had ever before experienced.

DEEP IMPRESSIONS

One afternoon I sat patiently awaiting my doctor's appointment when a woman walked into the waiting room with her newborn baby. We sat a few rows away from each other. I observed as she nestled her baby into the crook of her neck. During my twenty minute wait, I delighted in watching how she instinctively rocked and caressed her baby, impressing her deep love on this new soul.

Infants need to be stroked in order to mature into healthy toddlers. They need touch in order to know that they exist. As in the scene I witnessed with this new mother, we hope the quality of this touch for infants will be gentle and loving. If the touch is not or if the infant is left without contact, the infant will fail to grow and thrive. Similarly, to mature from our spiritual infancy our soul needs to be touched. That touch or contact can be a special event like falling in love, retirement or the birth of child. But it can also be the loss of a cherished relationship, a job or an injury that will cause a shift from our routine ways of perceiving life. When something meaningful "rocks the soul,"   momentum for change usually surfaces. It doesn't matter whether we interpret the event as positive or negative, what matters is what we do with the momentum created.

Many years ago, immediately following the birth of my daughter, I contracted a serious virus. The process of having a very difficult birth and being physically ill placed me in a delicate position and allowed for a sizable life shift. My personal health needs competed with the demands of my newborn child. I could only sustain the stress of this conflict for a short while before being pushed beyond my coping strategies. This experience was to be the first of a handful of life changing events that would teach me to recognize a call to get creative and grow.

What I remember most from this first big awakening was the feeling that everything had changed; nothing was familiar. It was obvious to me that my body was not the strong and agile body I knew so well. Exhaustion from illness and late night feedings took its toll. Somehow deep inside things were different. I was not thinking in the same way. I questioned the nature of my relationship with life. This restless situation demanded that I slow down and, with therapeutic support, feel my way through.

I would now identify this personal experience as a spiritual emergency because it quickly and intensely brought me to look inside. I was moved to begin redefining who I was and how I related to those forces of life that inspired me to touch into this restlessness and open to the deeper issues of my heart.

It is through these powerful moments that we are opened for a more soulful contact challenging us to begin a new relationship with life. Though it can be very mild as well, the nature of any impasse can provoke this. A spiritual emergency occurs when our identity dissolves significantly enough to create an existential distress. I like the term spiritual emergency for the term implies a need for immediate action in an unexpected situation. To my surprise I have found that within the impasse are all the elements needed to transform the sense of emergency into emerging opportunities.

A YEARNING AWAKENS

In the stories previously shared, we saw how yearnings awaken. Feelings of agitation become strong. Perceptions about life get stirred up. Momentum towards awareness builds, but it is still directionless and unfocussed. Like the light of a fire, this potential for awareness spreads out in all directions seeking to illuminate. As the intensity of this light expresses itself, all the individual will be aware of is the sense of agitation and yearning until the moment comes when something is reflected back. Here is when the intellect begins to take action. It uses the reflection as a small foothold, a link that allows the intellect to begin orienting the yearning towards its expression and fulfilment. It will continue to gather links until our senses feel satisfied that we have found the right balance for our specific spiritual needs.

My personal passage into motherhood awakened a yearning desire within me. The first reflections I received resonated a concern for nurturing and healing. While breastfeeding, I found it easy to bring my awareness inward, allowing time for reflection and resonance to increase in a natural way. As any woman who has breastfed may appreciate, there is a lot of time spent in the first year in this activity.

My transition into motherhood came with the added stressor of having contracted a serious virus, and this made my new life with baby very difficult. With regular visits with a naturopathic doctor I was introduced to herbal medicine. And here a whole new world opened up. I found myself powerfully intrigued by the nature of the healing arts. This was the first major reflection I received that moved me from my restless agitation into a more satisfying resonance with my new world. My curiosity piqued, I sought information about herbal medicine and the healing powers of plants through articles and books. Coincidentally a new acquaintance offered books on

Native spirituality and this began an insatiable, intellectual feeding frenzy. I couldn't get enough information. Through reading I immersed myself into a world I knew little about. This was a really fun and stimulating time. Not much was required of me. It was the perfect way to help me find spiritual frameworks for this profound yearning inside.

This passage was all about feeling and sensing my way. My impulses of desire and curiosity became my compass and pointed me towards immersion into books. My awakened intellect drove my thirst for knowledge, and found places where my imagination delighted in foreign ideas without any risk or danger. I entertained new concepts without any responsibility or commitment for any further action to be taken. The intense reading inspired a massive personal expansion, a snowballing effect that was being led by my own intuition and being framed within the context of the models my reading was providing.

In the spiritual context, the dynamic relationship between the intellect and the intuitive senses is being exercised and strengthened. The sensitivity and awareness of our unique spiritual language begins to develop. Like a child speaking words for the first time, our language is only in its early formative stages. We have clear evidence that we possess the means to develop it. Still at this stage all we can do is to discover and use preexisting models.

THE BEGINNERS MIND

Now that the intuitive senses and the intellect are in a relationship with each other, actively seeking, filtering and responding to new information – there is a budding presence of mind. This mind has an eagerly receptive and open quality and may be called the beginners mind. The quality of its receptivity is marked by its openly curious, observant, sensitive and innocent manner that is without judgement. It is of essential value at any stage of our path for it naturally can lead us to revelation.

Most often we consider the notion of mind as being the mental faculty of perception, yet today there is now greater acceptance that the term mind is referring to a field of perception that includes the sensory and emotional as well.

The beginner's mind is a naturally occurring, if unconscious, quality. It may be difficult to access after we have been imprinted with other models. We have to somehow relax and suspend the effect that our previous programming has on the quality of our receptivity.

A young woman in her mid-twenties described how her difficult circumstances brought her to understand and remember the beginners mind. She was an athlete as well as a highly gifted and accomplished martial artist. A svelte, agile and powerful woman who had spent 15 years of training to achieve the highest standings, she felt proud to define herself as a competitor at the international level. From an early age, she was conditioned to compare and compete with others as well as herself.

When on a trip with friends through the jungles of South America, she contracted a virus that made her deathly ill. Initially it seemed that this illness could be taken care of relatively easily through western medicine. With drugs many of the primary symptoms disappeared, but her vitality and core strength weren't recovering. The illness had weakened her badly and she couldn't get back to feeling well again. Over the next year she visited many doctors who could only tell her that there was nothing more to be done. Little prepared her for the shock of this life change that left her feeling perpetually tired and energy less.

A good friend suggested that she look into another form of martial art, something that had a focus on health and healing as a primary element. He believed that she might benefit from a physical process since she was such a kinaesthetic person. Perhaps she could try a medium that might feel familiar but not as demanding as her previous martial arts practice. Her resistance to this idea was a strong and resounding no – a clear negative. She had been a star, and with all her accomplishments she could not see herself being a beginner again. Starting all over would be very embarrassing and expose how weak and feeble she was. Only two years earlier she was strong and agile and she was furious that her life had changed.

Her resistance continued and so did the decline of her physical condition. She was so desperate to be well again and feel good in her body that eventually she decided go along with the idea and attend a few classes as a guest. Watching others in their ability to fully participate and seeing their healthy bodies in action, really hurt. All she could feel was her loss. She was stuck at an impasse.

The instructor was an older gentleman, who had spent much of his adult life teaching young people the subtle skills of internal martial arts. He was interested in fostering good health and conscious embodiment. So he approached this delicate situation with kindness and gentle compassion. Taking care to help her focus her attention and attend to the present moment, he gave her exercises that he felt certain she could accomplish. Through his care and consideration she slowly she began to relax.

He accepted her as she was, and she felt no judgement from him. This created an environment in which her internal argument could begin to decrease. She slowly stopped comparing herself with others and was now listening to his instruction. With her chattering mind now at rest, her beginners mind awakened once more. She felt still and quiet enough to enjoy the moment and to relish working with her body again. In time her healing process really took hold and her health began to return. What was once a dark and daunting situation was now a source of inspiration that brought her to understand and know a new power, one of compassion?

What this story illustrates is that new experiences naturally present the opportunity to meet the beginners mind by stimulating our attention. It also demonstrates how our rigid patterns can prevent us from cultivating new awareness and sensitivity. The beginners mind is not an easy state to maintain. When learning something new we are often preoccupied with our hunger to attain our goal and neglect to savour with consciousness the present moment. And again it is always at risk of being lost as we become familiar with routines and doze off into our comfy sleep-like state. Whether a newcomer to spiritual exploration, or as an "old comer" facing the delicate changes of other passages, to maintain this quality of mind demands that we remain humble and watchful that our tendencies towards achievement do not overpower us.

THE BRIDGE OF IMAGINATION

The unknown holds the ability to fascinate and terrify simultaneously. It's a delicate balance which direction we move towards. With the gathering of information from books, articles, blogs and discourse with others, the imagination is given spiritual frameworks in which to play. Here we can newly imagine ourselves and vicariously sense what our lives might be like within these situations.

The momentum of desire that opens in this second impasse has the potential to find focus within these imagined spiritual frameworks. Our curiosity will have clearer direction as it is transformed into fascination, more specifically directing our attention and attracting us into further exploration. The thirsty engine of our intuition and our intellect has now been kicked into high gear, and we look forward as the momentum continues to increase. What we previously sensed as raw feelings will begin to look for a more specific expression in our bodies as the fascination continues to build. Up to now we have been satisfied with the intellectual exercise of discovering spiritual models. Our intuition inspired this mental exercise. Now our imagination becomes the bridge that leads us towards a more tangible physical experience.

From the first impasse we saw the rumblings of change in the seeds of our awakening. Now we see the first steps towards acknowledging a personal interest and direction. This thirst for knowledge is an important step towards the mind's awakening and can be explored through any medium or discourse that offers a spiritual framework that intuitively resonates. This is a phase of inquiry that has great appeal because we get to play with options for our spiritual identity without any real consequence or responsibility. We continue in this preparatory phase until that time when we are ready for more experiential learning and commitment.

Chapter 3

The Search for Direct Experience

UP TO NOW WE HAVE BEEN GUIDED *by intuiting what feels right and appropriate for ourselves. Our attraction has been focussed through our fascination and our imagination has been gathering links for bridges yet to be built. The pull towards reading and intellectual discourse is still very appealing. Now there is the added calling for active physical*

participation. The power of the intellectual pursuit gains momentum. In the eagerness of our questioning, we seek a practical way that will lead us to tangible experiences of what we previously read about. We seek to find guidance in the context of a group and its ideology, with individual teachers or both.

This third impasse is characterized by the dabbler's dilemma, where by immersing ourselves briefly into a few spiritual models we mistakenly assume that this constitutes a full realization. The dilemma we face is the choice of either going deeper into the experiential processes for our learning or not. This is a challenge since we don't actually yet know what that process will entail – the unknown is still our companion.

SEEKING AND GATHERING

Commonly, the average person will spend four to seven years in formal post-secondary studies. Our culture puts great emphasis on the value of intellectual development and the gathering of information, and much less focus on spiritual process. The emphasis on gathering information promotes the birth of many spiritual seekers. These individuals who find great pleasure in the search itself and who take satisfaction in the discovery of frameworks that they sense, contain great power.

The beauty of seekers is that they have the drive and the ability to discover direction for their calling. This skill that they demonstrate will always be of good value. Seeking helps us to identify potential pathways. None-the-less, the seeker needs to be willing to slow down to produce awareness. Otherwise, the activity of the seeker is akin to a stone skipping and bouncing on the surface of the water without ever settling into the depths that lie just below.

The gap between the acquisition of information and the integration of that information through experience can be quite large. One way to bridge this gap is to use spiritual tools to access the depths within. Spiritual development encompasses much more than a glossary of terms and mental understandings; it requires that the heart be taken on a deep journey of relationship with self. Moving away from having just an intellectual grasp means engaging the whole self in the seeking, allowing for the enquiry to involve the senses, the body and the emotions.

SPIRITUAL TECHNOLOGY

Every spiritual tradition has its foundation of techniques designed to support an experiential understanding of the cosmology held within its system. The word technology refers to the use of tools and the study of techniques that are practiced in order to stimulate the body, mind and heart. Tools and practices are not necessarily the same thing. For example, over thousands of years the Ancient Hindu tradition has used mantras in its teaching of spirituality. The mantra is an example of a tool commonly used to still the mind. How we use that tool is referred to as a technique used in practice. Today anyone can go to a drop-in yoga class and hear the mantra Ohm, said to be the primordial sound of supreme consciousness. The word mantra means mind tool and refers to the use of sound syllables from the ancient Sanskrit language to create a resonance of light to focus the mind.

The main intention of using tools and techniques is to foster awareness that is grounded in experience. Many times this may also promote a sense of well-being, yet the most valuable spiritual aspect is the promotion of consciousness. Why? Because feelings, although powerful, are transient or impermanent; whereas, the consciousness that they can provoke is not.

Meditation as a technique is widely used as a way to calm and clear the body and mind in preparation for spiritual development. The process of meditating awakens a very special area of the brain called the prefrontal cortex. This area of the brain is located at the forehead and is said to be responsible for the regulation of emotion, empathy, insight and much more. When the prefrontal cortex is activated there can be a harmonizing and stabilizing effect with all other parts of the brain. This is excellent news for anyone looking to reduce stress and develop greater compassion.

When inducing a meditative state through spiritual practice, the prefrontal cortex plays an important role because it supports our awareness to go beyond our day to day frame of mind, which can lead us to new levels of consciousness. Note: not all meditation practices are alike nor create the same results. Different types of meditation bring on different effects that awaken and stimulate different qualities of intensity in the brain and body. Therefore, it is important to know your technology, or have good guidance to avoid bumps and bruises.

One of my good friends was really delighted to find that she could retrieve so much free information off the internet. She downloaded a whole course in order to learn a particular spiritual practice and worked on it intently for many long hours. She was having a great time, it was easy stuff to do that she knew little about and she was keenly interested. All went well until she had a grave experience. Somehow the practices triggered all kinds of distortions. Her anxiety levels went through the roof. Her doctor could not help her in anyway concrete other than to offer her a sedative. My friend was at a loss. She learnt a valuable lesson that clarified for her the truth that spiritual tools have great power and that she didn't presently have the wisdom to know how to "play" with this power on her own. This outcome nevertheless gave her enough experience to know that what came forward from the practice wasn't just random. It was personal material that needed to be addressed with consideration.

The attraction to using a technique happens because we want to improve our quality of life. We want to feel calmer, happier. We want to feel good so we take on a practice with the hopes of creating some specific results. Sometimes this works well. The experience will be enjoyable enough and we are drawn to continue. When first establishing a relationship with tools and techniques, often beginners will enjoy the wonder of a new practice until the novelty wears off and then the real work starts. The process of spiritual development necessitates a consistency in practice that can be challenging to maintain after the initial excitement wears off. It is then we begin to see the real effort it takes for a meaningful spiritual practice to develop. This can be a snag for many people who don't yet know how to continue to apply themselves when the fun and attraction shifts to discomfort and resistance.

As we begin to progress, we have to learn that meeting resistance is a regular part of the work and requires discipline. The argument that resistance presents us with can be quite strong and the effort involved to work through it can be demanding and may temporarily feel stressful. Often the time in the day allotted for practice is when we most want to rest and so it becomes an arduous task to sit and apply ourselves. We want the fruit of the practice, but haven't yet developed the staying power to meet the argument that our resistance presents. This may be felt as fatigue, distress, boredom, disillusionment and even anger. Because of this, we may feel justified in dropping the practice since it was intended to make us feel better. We can rationalize this by thinking that we have tried it and know what it's about, when in fact we have only a conceptual understanding for it takes at least ninety days of consistent practice to establish a new pattern.

When I was young, I decided that I would learn meditation and committed to a simple practice I had taken from a book. All that was asked was five minutes of my day. I really didn't know what I was doing. Having struggled with its application for the better part of a year, I was astounded that this could be so difficult. Later I learned that though some stages are tough, it's not meant to be so difficult. I had to learn the hard way that the form I had chosen was just inappropriate for me. Each of us has a different way of learning and growing. I finally achieved success with meditation when I found the right guidance and practices that appealed to my senses. Then the learning and practicing became fun and easy.

As we apply ourselves to a regular practice, it's inevitable that we meet with stages of discomfort. Feelings, thoughts and body symptoms will begin vying for attention. This can feel like a distraction when in fact it signals that the process of change has begun. Our work is to allow this process and feel our way through by paying attention and staying with the flow. The simplicity of this may be deceiving. The process may be simple but it is not easy to remain consistent in practice. In face of this challenge we have to engage ourselves with kind consideration. This will leave a lasting impression in our own hearts that will reflect outwardly in positive ways. Every stage of our spiritual growth will help deepen our emotional intelligence and strengthen the bridge of relationship with life. Practice that makes life more engaging, more enjoyable will benefit everyone. I consider any activity that supports awareness and consciousness of heart to be a spiritual practice and doesn't have to have a formal application.

STUMBLING WITH SELF-IMPORTANCE

With any impasse, questions arise that cause us to reassess our underlying intentions. Though we would like to think that those first stages that inspire us to learn practice are motivated by an altruistic desire to do service, it may be shocking to know that this may not be the total truth. The average person moves through life bumping along, seeking fulfilment motivated by essential needs: the need for security, the need for personal power, the need to be loved etc...These primary needs fuel our motivation more than any altruistic action.

An altruistic action is one that acts unselfishly for the welfare of others. Spiritual activity can express itself that way, but it is by far not the only motivation. Even if we believe our motivation to be purely altruistic, spiritual practice will eventually reveal that our own ego may have more to do with it than we might be able to see at first. This is not to say that the actions we take do not also include a desire to do service for others. The practice process will naturally reveal a more complete picture of the needs underlying our motivations.

If you have ever had the feeling of being "busted", as if someone just took a spot light and focussed it on the most unsophisticated part of you, then you know the feeling of an exposed ego. When this happens we feel so vulnerable. Operating with an agenda of which the rules are usually unspoken and unavailable, our ego doesn't like that others see what we are really up to – not even ourselves. So it takes good care to not expose itself, playing a very subtle game under different disguises. It can masquerade as sweet and friendly, meanly cruel, innocently daft or brilliant and intelligent. The point is that our ego attempts to be in charge of the process of preserving our self-image, hoping to maintain control of the ship and steer things to benefit this agenda. Its motive is practical: to protect and secure. Our ego does this routinely by implementing the repetition of patterns: actions and behaviours that need little or no thought. Once again we see the power of those basic imprints we have acquired in survival training as we grew up.

In spiritual terms, these self-focussed motivations are called self-importance. As mentioned, the nature of their activity is to maintain self-image at all cost, concealing and inhibiting the expansion of our awareness, supporting our robotic patterns. So here we come full circle and, once more, have to watch out for those actions that we repeat without consciousness. This will be a constant requirement throughout our life development.

This self-important behaviour is both subtle and strong. It can hide itself in our internal dialogues with personal justifications that reason away or close off any ability to hear information that does not support its agenda. It characterizes itself with judgemental attitudes like pride, arrogance and fear that support a self-image of being better or worse than another.

The ego is fiercely protective of the self and borrows its energy from our survival instincts. Whenever the ego's sense of security feels threatened we might react with feelings of discomfort, anger, fear, vulnerability or distress to name a few. In extreme reaction to threat we can feel like we are falling apart, sometimes literally, even to the point of wondering if we will physically die as we experience symptoms like palpitations, shortness of breath, perspiration and muscular tremors.

SPIRITUAL EGO

Spiritual practice can naturally induce an awareness of our repressed or distorted thoughts and feelings. Like in polishing silverware we are exposed to those areas that need polishing. Our spiritual practice polishes the self, touching and exposing the brilliance of our potential, our true nature.

In awakening to our true nature every stage of our growth will reveal an equally subtle "dark and selfish" aspect, meaning that we are living a perpetual dance of opposites throughout this life span. The further along we are on the path, the more subtle is the challenge to see the shadow of self-importance. Therefore, it is simply naïve at any stage of development to assume that we have arrived, or will arrive at and maintain a utopian life free of self-importance. The wheel of life turns constantly. Change is the only predictable thing we have. Even as we mature we will always encounter transitions. Each transition we go through is like a little death that penetrates our mind's delusions, simultaneously deepening our awareness. Acceptance of this perpetual dance of opposites helps to maintain a clear focus for creating a positive outcome through the difficult impasses to come.

The ego charges into play when we are unwilling to accept this dance of opposites. There is nothing more disturbing than spiritual arrogance. How often, in the name of love, are actions taken with underlying attitudes of contempt, judgement, greed or fear. This is a negative consequence to having accumulated spiritual power without having understood the cornerstone of Heart. Truly understanding and accepting that self-importance is always at play, helps in relating to spiritual power with caution and care. Addressing our self-importance will help to alleviate obstacles that can cause much suffering. When we consider what motivation is behind our desires and impulses, we can take more intentional actions. In keeping with this awareness there is then the possibility of service with humility and sincere equanimity.

In my experience, no one is exempt from, nor beyond challenges of this kind. Having witnessed many circumstances involving myself and others, I have been astonished by the ego's drive.

THE WONDER AND CHALLENGE

When the time is right, our desire for spiritual knowledge will draw us to the outside world to find a guide or teacher. It can feel like a daunting task to navigate the plethora of information available when accessing mainstream spirituality. Like nothing we could have ever imagined, there are so many options now available for our spiritual interests. With internet and social media, we are given multicultural possibilities and many potential pathways. We are blessed to have the freedom to inform ourselves and to explore a spiritual path of whatever flavour we choose. During this time of spiritual globalization, there are many options for introductory levels of study. We now have the privilege of dabbling and taste testing. We can check things out, do a drop-in yoga class, a weekend meditation retreat, or practice some martial arts. These are ways that can help us get our senses more deeply involved with our exploration.

Although having access to all of this information is wonderful, it is important to understand that ancient spiritual teachings have been adapted and watered down for mainstream consumption. This does not always translate into good practice or good teaching. Today a person can find a degree of aptitude with a spiritual modality and within a short period of time become a teacher. Programs create their own certification standards by generalizing terminology, concepts and practices and synthesizing the material for mass application. On the one hand to have easy access to abundant information may seem great, yet that easy access can lead to a lack of depth in teaching and limit the degree of personal transformation.

Traditionally a student would be given practices and taken through a series of experiences over many years. This is a process where trials and initiations would refine the development of awareness, and consciousness of heart. Only then after a substantial amount of time, dedication, and practice would a person have enough experience to safely and consciously guide others through change and uncertainty in the unknown.

More than ever we have popular culture "advertising" spiritual growth with short term trainings that give enough to inform but not to transform. New students will likely receive their first teachings from someone who will have little real life experience. This may simply be a reflection of the times, where today's young student gets to dabble in a wading pool of entry level practices as a way to engage and sample without much consequence. Lamentably, this creates a world of mediocrity with the effect of promoting confusion rather than setting a path of distinction. The student may also then have difficulty recognising what to look for when the need for deeper explorations arise.

I recall meeting with Angela, a 30 year old woman who had recently finished her masters degree in sociobiology. Angela was keenly interested in all things spiritual. When she introduced herself, it was clear that she had done lots of reading. She had all the lingo, but could tell me little of how this information was to help support her at this present time. Angela was suffering from feeling seriously directionless and spiritually ungrounded. In spite of her brilliance and intelligence, all she could do was attempt to synthesise the information she had gathered. This created a potent cocktail of mixed concepts that acted like a spiritual depressant, confusing her and making her ill. She was now preparing to enter the world as a professional and was struggling as she faced this darkness.

Angela held the misunderstanding that more is better. In her mind she thought that exposure to more spiritual information meant she would be healthier and happier. Here she presented the classic challenge of following the mainstream flow by immersing herself in lots of spiritual "stuff". She felt this might remedy the anxiety she had about entering the professional world. What this actually created was a lot of confusion, with little direction. She had done lots of surface exploration, and none of it actually helped her manage her underlying stress. What she needed was guidance in how to apply the precious tools she had acquired.

OF SPIRITUAL TEACHERS AND HEALERS

The true purpose of a spiritual teacher is to sit by the water with us until we want to get wet, and share with us the principles of swimming. Up to now we've been sitting by the water, reading and contemplating about immersing ourselves.

The spiritual experience is individual and the readiness to immerse ourselves is not something we can predict in a certain time frame. When we are ready we search for someone who will assist us. It can be a challenge to find a good teacher, one that will suit our learning style, someone who has the right personality and the skills to take us through to the steps.

Over the many years I have had some loving and impeccable teachers and healers. Dedicated men and women who have given of their knowledge and time and, through example, have made the teachings simple and accessible. And then there are those teachers with whom I have learnt about the m ore painful side of the student teacher exchange. These have been stressful circumstances that have brought forward reflections of early childhood trauma. Either way, it has been a valuable exercise in learning about growth choices. I prefer the more sensitive, loving and direct way of caring.

The caring and compassionate way teaches us to have empathy for our own suffering as well as the suffering of others. I regard this as a crucial quality for compassion and caring opens the door for clearer perceptions of what connects us in relationship to the world. The field of unification for those connections to be made is what I call Heart. Heart is the cornerstone that provides stability for greater humanism in our social interconnection. Although the concept is simple, it holds a rich complex of power that adds to our driving force for spiritual growth. Some of the qualities within this field are: tenderness, sensitivity, kindness, understanding, clarity, strength, integrity, acceptance, receptivity, flexibility, caring and humility. In this third impasse we have an inclination to look for tools, or ways to tap into this field and for people who might help us do that. This is intuitively driven.

The teacher who is intimately aware of how the ego inevitably affects the process, and who holds this field of Heart as a priority, is apt to bring an abundance of wisdom and care for the student's journey. The clear motivation of the spiritual teacher is to help the student foster freedom from ego and attachments and find true consciousness of Heart.

I recommend looking for someone who inspires curiosity, helps articulate questions, and points in directions where answers might be discovered. Otherwise, if our questioning is continuously appeased with answers from another, we can come to depend on answers from outside and miss the opportunity to discover how to make connections for ourselves. Without meeting the challenge of making our own connections, we cannot take responsibility for our own choices and actions. It's a huge loss when we put time, energy and money into this journey and yet fail to discover ourselves.

Today we are inundated with flashy, powerful and exciting spectacles for our entertainment, and tend to look for stimulating situations. In doing so, we may overlook the enduring and simple qualities of a kind and humble teacher. Following a teacher who has impressive power and high capacities for spiritual knowledge can be especially fun. And though their extraordinary abilities may set them apart, this does not necessarily make them a good teacher. It is easy to be drawn to someone who can create dramatic effects, but this may be a smoke screen for the true unveiling. So it is not how they look, or how much they can impress us that will tell us if this person is a good match.

For years I witnessed a colleague go through a continual push and pull with this hook. Sheryl was an intelligent woman in her mid-forties with an established career in engineering. An avid reader who enjoyed attending all kinds of spiritual gatherings and trainings, she received many techniques and practices to support her spiritual development. Given that Sheryl's primary interest was in understanding how things worked, she loved the exposure to different models and structures. She was very honest to say she was much less comfortable with doing the practices.

Over the years, she followed her interest in this way, dotting around the globe going to "power spots," acquiring knowledge and eventually gravitated towards the world of phenomena and the paranormal. She travelled far and wide to be involved with powerful "psychic healers." Sheryl was attracted to the freaky, frightening and exciting world of spirits, ghosts and other phenomena. She was eager to learn and understand her spiritual world from this point of view, and was fascinated with the world of psychics, and the techniques they used. This was fun in the beginning but later it all turned into a bit of nightmare, for more than ever before, she became lost and confused about her own identity. She became plagued with growing concerns over ghosts and demons. And she had never developed any real sense of personal power. Most of her spare time was devoted to managing her fears with less time for living, laughing and growing.

It is a common misunderstanding to think that those who are gifted with esp or psychic capabilities will have a high degree of spiritual intelligence. The challenge we face with the world of psychics as with healers is to understand that each of them work within their own system of filters, their unique view of reality or personal paradigm. That someone can see or speak with angels, spirits and ghosts suggests that some of their faculties may be developed, and that a measure of their awareness is set with these features.

To know and learn that phenomena exists is for some an important part of the waking journey. It really is a wonder that nature can present such strange and compelling experiences, but this does not mean that a person who enjoys working in this way will also have the capacity to maintain clarity, wisdom and heartcentredness to adequately lead others on their spiritual journey.

Our exposure to this world is usually from a distance; through reality TV shows, movies and other media presenting this area of life as very exciting. My sense is that Sheryl was having a lot of fun until she awakened from her cocoon and realized that it was time to approach her spiritual life with more consciousness. By extricating herself from her entanglement with the world of strange happenings, she could now grow and benefit from this involvement by better knowing herself. Her trials offered her valuable learning and moved her into a new level of intimacy with her spiritual process. She was now inspired to use the tools she already had to help her enjoy a more balanced life.

An effective teacher knows how to support an individual through their process of transformation by providing tools, experience and strategies in a compassionate manner. They understand that if they are successful in their job, then they will likely make themselves redundant.

Teachers need students and students need teachers, and together they grow until it is time for them to part. The spiritual student will likely experience many teachers in their lifetime. There is no single way to say how to find a good teacher yet I hope the qualities I have mentioned above will assist in this. It is assured that the student will be given the opportunity to clarify what they need with every teacher that they work with.

In conclusion this passage is a delicate stage of developing a personal communication system that is based upon a desire to find existing models in the outside world that will adequately express our spiritual longing. We seek tools and spiritual techniques that can create a bridge to the field of unification that is our Heart – the cornerstone for greater humanism in our social interconnection.

What motivates our longing for the spiritual path may be something that looks good and benevolent, but underlying this may be something more power oriented and ego driven. We have to negotiate the shadow of our self-importance and navigate the plethora of watered down information found in mainstream spirituality to avoid the dabbler's dilemma. To do so we are challenged to make our own heartfelt connections and seek out teachers who inspire our curiosity, help articulate our questions, and point us in directions where we may discover our own answers. A connection between a teacher and student that holds consciousness of the ego and its attachments will expose the student's brilliant potential through cultivating true consciousness of heart. And if the teacher has cultivated true openness of heart, there will be a direct reflection in the laying of a sound foundation for mindful observation. For the student, this sets the course for a positive outcome as more challenging transitions occur.

Chapter 4

The Dark Night of the Senses

HAVING NOW EXPLORED POSSIBLE AVENUES *for self- fulfilment, we begin to sense the joy that a spiritual path can provide. Our desire to realize this inspires us to unite with others of like mind and follow a devotional process. Here we commit to our spiritual growth through a purposeful practice. This commitment is the first of two aspects in this fourth transition. It rekindles the innocence with which we came into this world and opens us to a euphoric*

*presence of Heart. We gain new range of freedom
and increased willingness to devote to the focus of
our exploration. This is a delightful part of the passage, a place we may want to linger in for some time.
When we reach the 2nd part of this passage; we
meet what is called the Dark Night of the Senses.
This is symptomized by a deep cleansing and release
of outdated perceptions that will no longer serve
us. Our senses begin a transformative process of
disengaging anything that is not resonant with the
euphoric qualities that have captured us. This brings
to light any of our darker perceptions and presents
us with the first real experience of self-perception
that is in opposition to that which we so fervently
desire.*

ENTRANCED BY LOVE

When I was a teenager my older sister was married in our
village chapel. This was a very quaint, little, white chapel
with stained glass windows. The scene was picturesque
and inspired feelings of beauty, safety, and community.
It was a perfect setting through which to experience a
sense of union, love and harmony.

This scene gives an example of what inspires the feeling that attracts us into committing ourselves to deeper
spiritual process and leads us into this fourth passage.
This occurs when our intellectual needs have been sat-

isfied enough to allow our attraction to this feeling to take us into further experiential exploration.

This first part is like the honeymoon phase of a delicious love affair: everything feels good; everything feels right. Devoting time to service and practice feels effortless. Offering ourselves for the higher good supports our vision. Now there is direct payback, for through our actions there is discernible support that tells us we are on track for ourselves. The resource of positive feedback, whether through community or a natural consequence of our own intuition, helps to strengthen a trust that we have made a good choice. Our perception of this breeds a comfort and we abandon ourselves to it with the hopes of a journey filled with love. We might feel that for the first time we have come home. We belong and all is good. The feelings of wellness and joy reflect to us that this path will bring the security we have always longed for. This enhances our commitment to it.

This first stage will likely move us to disclose to the world our affinity with being a spiritual aspirant. For some, the calling might cause them to make choices that go well beyond their normal way, inciting them to break free of their culturally recognised lifestyle. By choosing a more alternative or extreme spiritual path, friends and family might view this transformation as a little insane. Yet for the aspirant, the imperative is to manifest creative spiritual expression; something they feel is in alignment with their need for spiritual fulfil-ment. Some may go as far as to completely renounce their worldly ways in order to freely relish in their spir-itual passion.

Also though not common, some people do have the disposition and attitude that will secure them in a mode of expression that allows for this first stage of experi-ence to be the platform through which they live their entire spiritual life.

Here is the story of Adrian who travelled abroad to study architecture. He was completely enamoured with old European architectural styles and wanted to create beautiful modern structures from ancient models, he never imagined how this journey would change his spir-itual life.

During his initial year, he relished his studies but found he was lonely. Having always had trouble making friends, he struggled with the same old social fears. The only person he felt any closeness with was a professor with whom he would sometimes have tea and talk about his love for architecture.

One rainy afternoon, during one of these visits, his teacher shared a little bit more about his personal life, telling him of his passion for Buddhism. Adrian hav-ing been brought up without any spiritual life, had lit-tle exposure to Buddhist philosophy. Yet he was curious and followed his intrigue engaging his professor in more dialogue on the subject. Many passionate discussions ensued and eventually his professor invited him to visit with a good friend of his who happened to also be a Tibetan Lama.

Something unusual happened that day when the Lama, the teacher and the student came together. As if a fire ignited, they spent many hours discussing and debating theological issues. Never would it have crossed Adrian's mind that he would befriend these two men. A strong bond developed between them and led to weekly get-togethers. In time Adrian visited the local Buddhist temple, and it became the place where the three would gather on a regular basis.

Without any spiritual background, he felt conflicted by his draw to Buddhism, yet found he could not deny himself the strong attraction. When he returned home for visits, he never disclosed any of this with his family. Upon his returns to Europe he was eager to pursue his interest with abandonment. With time he could no longer deny his passion and recognised his need to immerse himself completely. It was a total shock for his parents to learn that Adrian had decided to immerse himself in a 3 year Buddhist renunciation program.

Adrian had become entranced. The circumstances ignited feelings he had never encountered before. He felt closer to himself and also connected to a world that awakened his passion and love for life on a greater scale. What took hold in him was a powerful passion for his spiritual development, and for now, his honeymoon was in full bloom.

THE DARK NIGHT OF THE SENSES

Our delicious love affair and our euphoric feelings create such a powerful filter over our perceptions that for a time it can paint everything we see and make it all as picturesque as the lovely chapel I first spoke of. This provides us with the ability to view the potential of how the world could be governed with love and how we can be a part of manifesting this consciousness in a worldly way.

But, little by little there is a subtle transition that will occur. As the heart opens we can see more, feel more and sense more. We open to feel not only the passion but the pain as well, and so the dance between the polarities begins. We want to see the world in a fixed way and maintain the visions of love and beauty. Yet we can no longer deny the disillusionment that arises through our awareness of pain and suffering.

The awareness that we are able to project such an idealistic vision brings with it a bitter sweet experience. We see and feel the wonder and power of love. We also begin to recognise that we are projecting this vision on our world. In doing this are we not then looking at the world through rose coloured glasses? Like the Red Queen in Alice in Wonderland are we painting the roses red? Through our attraction to the sparkle of love have we fallen in love with the idea of love? Now begins a sense of disillusionment. Along with it emerges the struggle to maintain the feelings of wonder and power we've become so strongly attracted to.

Having been so inspired by the pleasure and appeal for love and devotion, it's a shock that things begin to change. This churns up all kinds of questions about the nature of our choices, our relationships and our motivations. Once the disillusionment begins to filter through, we become attuned to seeing the lovely red paint peeling off the roses. This is perplexing and will bring into question if it is truly love that is guiding us. Our quest to maintain our vision soon gives us the intuitive sense that the power of love may be much more than we could have imagined.

In the beginning little discrepancies will pop up. These create a gap between what we feel and what we want to feel. Tension builds and that serves as a catalyst to help bring these gaps into awareness. Making preparation for the Dark Night of the Senses is like preparing for the delivery of baby. One can only prepare in a conceptual way. When the real experience occurs it is marked with a power that feels undeniably beyond our control.

Let's look at the term Dark Night of the Senses. This darkness is a metaphor for what feels like a lens dimming and even blackening our usual way of viewing life. The nature of this darkness feels initially blinding. It slows us down and provokes a shift from our habitual patterns and perceptions. The reference to night implies touching the shadow life of our soul. We are awakened to pre-existing conflicts and what we so readily deny in ourselves.

The reference to the Senses refers to the pathways though which we connect with life. Our sense of sight, taste, hearing, touch and smell become distorted with what we deem to be distasteful and unacceptable. There is repulsion to feeling this way, so we try to pull away. This only creates more pain. We don't want to feel and we can't think our way out of this one. This dark night affects our routines and assumptions about how life is supposed to be, we don't see with the same eyes, we don't hear with same ears, our sense of taste has gone bitter - the bodies senses have shifted and feel contorted with discomfort.

This term "Dark Night of Senses" was coined by Theresa of Avila and St-John of the Cross whose writings have been foundational in furthering our understanding of spiritual transformation. They describe this passage as something totally pervasive, a movement of conscious-ness that is mystically driven and which penetrates the fabric of who we are.

Impasses exaggerate those gaps in our psyche, they really make us aware of our dual nature - the push and pull between the known and the unknown, the good and the bad. This transition is full of intensity, like meeting up with the impossible and feeling no way to manoeuvre, it can be an experience of deep suffering with no relief from the torment until we relax, accept the circumstances and stop fighting .

Since this impasse can take its own sweet time with us, sometimes taking many moons to move us through an unrecognizable filtering of the senses, the mind is full of quandary. This process is ignited and directed by something we are not conscious of, so our mind has no structure to contain it. Evaluating is pointless since it doesn't make clear sense. The only solution here is to observe without attachment– just pay attention, although that is more easily said than done.

Writer psychologist, Thomas Moore describes this type of impasse as an expression and cry of the soul, that deep and distinct part of us that aspires for expansion, growth and realization. The soul engages its forces to describe in a sensorial way our human experience as a paradox, this necessitates that we adopt a way of evaluating that is free of judgement.

Based on fears of losing what little control we seem to have, our tendency is to hold and resist. This resistance attempts to coerce us into believing that if we allow this darkness then we will no longer exist – we don't want to experience anything other than the light!...

Curiously, what is happening can actually serve to free us from what we are refusing to accept in ourselves. The messy fact is that, in the spiritual way of relating, the shadow serves to tell us that we have begun a remapping of the senses. It is a time to come clean with whatever we are denying or hiding. The essence of this stage is to sift through our deep core so that we get acquainted with behaviours, attitudes, feelings that we may be unaware of and which lack harmony with the path we have chosen. This is the way our divine nature insists upon equanimity in our relationship to the polarities we perceive in life.

STORY OF ONE

Sometimes we remain in the honeymoon stage of this transition for a very long time before we come to the Dark Night of the Senses, and sometimes we get the shock of our lives and come to the experience of this great cleansing from the get-go.

I was introduced to a young woman who had recently returned from a journey to India where she had met a renowned Guru. She was fresh out of college and her journey had been one to celebrate her newly found freedom from school. This was her first experience travelling away from home, so it was quite a cultural shock to suddenly find she was seated in front of the Guru, an acclaimed spiritual figure who was said to be the reincarnation of a spiritual saint.

She was totally enchanted by the lively spiritual scene: the sea of devotees dressed in colourful flowing outfits, the chanting, the wild dancing that created an air of community and heightened ecstasy. Her description of this scene was like something out of a story book

At that time she could not have been happier. The daily routines and rituals were easy to follow, the highlight of which was to sit in meditation with the Guru and receive his teachings and blessings.

Over the course of a few months, she noticed feeling like she was under the influence of some sort of love drug for she felt a high that didn't go away. Yet this was all natural. She was certain that she had found her calling and was so happy to be part of this community she began making plans to extend her visit.

Then she had an experience that she would always remember. One day while sitting quietly, listening to the Guru's chanting, she instinctively raised her head to look at him. To her surprise their gaze locked together for a few moments, the energy that she felt course through her entire body was electrifying.

The experience was so profound that it left her feeling disoriented. It touched the depths of her mind in such a way that she felt extreme lightness. Her immediate response was to laugh and then cry. Her behaviour was outside of the norm and she couldn't control herself. What followed was a flood of sadness, fears and depression. Her experience in India had dramatically shifted from euphoria to a dark emotional state that it seemed nothing could alter. Her experience in India had shifted; she was catapulted into a process of cleansing and healing.

This young woman had moved rapidly from the honeymoon phase into a Dark Night. Her difficulty was that she was unprepared to suddenly meet up with the deep feelings, some of which were painful.

It's often shocking to know that questing for goodness and kindness can reveal to us a very dark underbelly, requiring that we find courage and strength. Learning to treat our shadowy self with tenderness is the biggest lesson here. So many people grow up ignoring these difficult feelings because they aren't given the tools, or allowed the space for the healthy expression of their power and intensity. Their mobilization is a beautiful gift because powerful emotion is a primary ingredient that is essential for our spiritual growth. This enhances our ability to connect with our empathic nature, and makes it possible for us to develop greater levels of sensitivity and loving capacity.

OF FEELINGS, FAITH, AND COMMITMENT
Feelings
When we are presented with the gift of mobilizing our ability to feel and sense, we are faced with the dilemma of whether we want to accept the gift or not. We can sense the potency of its contents to such a degree that we shy away because our primal response is that this may be dangerous. Although the ability for feeling is basic to our system it is not an easy thing to accept.

Surprisingly, many people don't know how to accept or manage their feelings. Poet E.E. Cummings describes this well when he says about feeling... "may sound easy.

It isn't. A lot of people think or believe or know they feel—but that's thinking or believing or knowing; not feeling".

Fundamentally, feeling is not thinking, at least not with the rational mind. We need to cultivate the sensorial mind. This way of thinking is so instinctual to us that it is challenging to bring it to consciousness. The language of the felt senses or somatic thinking is felt physically and emotionally. It is immediate and pervasive and can easily overtake rational perception. It is so closely linked with our primal response systems that we can easily be inspired to take action upon it before we have time to think rationally.

This is a gift we all have yet harnessing it into conscious intention is more than a simple task. It takes faith to take the next step of learning to trust this language of the felt senses. It can be likened to culture shock where everything you know is no longer applicable and your ability to communicate is severely impaired. Until we have integrated its contents every sensory signal may be screaming that we run and return to what is familiar. If we do run back to the familiar landscape we will lose the opportunity for expanding consciousness and emotional range.

This is the impasse. It is marked by strong feelings and perceptions, mainly interpreted as difficult or negative. The leap here is one of faith. The task is to stand firm in face of the powerful desire to get away from the discomfort and sustain ourselves in the new environment until we can integrate a new understanding.

Developing the willingness to feel does require courage. Our system of patterns usually comes with many default settings. These are ways that we side step what is really happening to keep the old program intact. Nothing wants to die; especially old emotional and mental programs that we've come to believe are secure or designed to keep us safe and cosy.

The Question of Faith

Faith is the foundational framework within which we can sustain ourselves when meeting the unknown. In fact we can't discover what faith is without meeting the unknown directly. Traditionally faith is spoken of in relation to a philosophy or religion. Yet consider that faith is, at its root, the ability to take committed action without knowing the outcome. It bridges and embraces our connection to a spiritual process. Without this bridge we will lack consciousness in our spirituality. Faith transcends both our sensorial and rational minds and allows for unknown potential to present itself.

The origin of the word faith comes from the Greek Goddess of trust, whose name was Fides. She was a good spirit who escaped the opening of Pandora's Box by fleeing to heaven. Pandora's Box was said to contain all the evils in the world, and when the all-gifted Pandora opened the box, Fides fled to heaven opening the gateway with divine consciousness. Through this ancient Greek myth we are presented with the question of whether we can go beyond trust and have faith; distilling from our hearts those heavenly qualities that will allow us to maintain right relationship when our world is in chaos.

To consider faith is also to consider a simple act of being with Heart and not shut down in face of the painful or unknown. This asks that we stand loyally in our centre, like the eye of the hurricane, maintaining a grounded presence as things unfolds around us. Through our faith we can learn to see that divine forces present a world that is not fixed or solid, a world of infinite possibilities.

Commitment

Faith introduces us to the great strength and ability we have to commit. We are now in a position to discover how we may wish to use this ability with consistent intention. For our journey through the unknown in this passage, in one way or another, we develop practices that support presence, heart and will. This may be done through a focus on simple attitudes and processes or through complex spiritual traditions. As faith reveals commitment, commitment helps to build faith. Through a practice in which the power of faith and commitment are present we may form an unshakeable foundation for spiritual development.

INTENTION AND CAUSATION

Up to now we've been discussing the emergence of a natural desire towards spiritual development and the fact that actively engaging in this process will bring with it challenging transitions that we have called impasses. In this fourth impasse the strength of our attraction to the feelings for comfort, joy, connection and love has surfaced naturally and brought us to shocking revelations about our own nature and the challenges of dualistic perception. The discomfort factor creates a junction of choice. Here we can decide to go back to what is familiar or investigate beyond. This brings us more closely to the issue of intention and how intention plays a big role in our development.

Should we decide to continue with our quest towards kindness, empathy and equanimity, we will meet the requirement of strengthening our resolve to take committed action even in the face of great discomfort. The next decision is to consider how we might do this. Once again our search for support and guidance will be an issue. If we have already found a teacher and a practice then our commitment to them will increase. If not, then there is an urgency to discover the best foundation through which to grow.

Through committed practice comes the inevitable understanding how this intentional action will bring with it great personal change and challenge. This heightens our awareness of the relationship between cause and effect. Any committed action produces an effect.

One of the common effects is that committed spiritual practice will awaken our memory systems to a whole new level and begin reacquainting us with previously unconscious material. Our memory is a complex system of interactive association that constantly modifies itself. Whenever we are remembering, we are either reinforcing or altering a perception. This gives us an opportunity to consider intentionally altering our perceptions rather than reinforcing old ones.

Intentional action with spiritual practice may be taken in various ways. For the spiritual practitioner this means a dedicated approach that includes routine practice. For others this may bring them to make use of other means such as way to shift from consensual reality. For example, the use of medicinal power plants has been historically practiced in various shamanic traditions for their assistance in opening us to different dimensions of consciousness.

SANTA AND HIS FLYING REINDEER

I was walking past a nearby school yard one beautiful fall afternoon. Drawn to peek over the chain link fence, I saw under a majestic cedar tree a clump of mushrooms. These were not your ordinary mushrooms – I was in awe. These were bright red with white spots. My mind raced back, recalling the many times I had seen these toadstools mushrooms in story books and depicted in fairy tale stories.

Someone else had also spotted them. We were both standing there wide eyed looking at the magical red mushrooms whose name is Amanita Muscaria. A poisonous mushroom found in the more temperate areas of the northern hemisphere, they have a wide history of influence in spiritual growth. This mushroom contains a substance that is said to have been ingested by Siberian shamans to achieve an alternate state of awareness.

These bright red and white circular mushrooms were supposedly first given to a sacrificial reindeer. The animal would ingest the substance thereby filtering a large portion of the poisonous chemical out, thus leaving the distilled psychoactive component in the reindeer's urine which the shaman would drink. The shaman would then pass his urine to others, supporting them in safely inducing an alternate state of consciousness. This folkloric bit of history gave birth to the myth of the flying reindeer and the image of Santa Clause – the shaman dressed in red and white, delivering good things to all who were good.

Poisonous plant organisms like this Amanita Muscaria are also called power plants and have been used as a sacred way by shamans and healers throughout history for the awakening and renewal of consciousness. These power plants are said to have a spirit, an active consciousness that guides us through a shift in perception, hopefully leading to a soothing and harmonizing of spirit. In most cases, this will only happen once we have first given up and purged what obstructs our awareness.

Plant medicine can be used to induce or simulate a "Dark Night of the Senses" pushing the recipient to let go of limiting perceptions or beliefs that induce soul sickness. It is now more common in the west to see the use of power plants as a way to actively seek spiritual growth.

Though power plants can stimulate and bring on an impasse by actively pushing the psyche into expanded awareness, it is advisable that this be done with proper guidance and mindfulness. Any substance used to assist our spiritual growth will have the effect of energetically altering our filters of perception. If our system is taken energetically too far beyond our ability to reintegrate the consciousness received we may be left feeling lost and in great distress.

And so to help avoid such pitfalls it is important to realize that daily living is our primary gateway for spiritual development. How to educate, stimulate and grow in awareness through gradual, consistent and respectful application offers a strong foundation through which to filter and integrate difficult events brought forward during big transitions.

In conclusion the Dark Night of the Senses is a humbling time that sets us up for a larger momentum of change. We are stimulated to look down the deep well and take a good look at our poisonous attitudes and tendencies, at whatever obstacles or attachments that limit us from maintaining clear and loving awareness.

Although it is perhaps strange we have to meet these difficult impasses, as is the way with nature, we are continually presented with the dynamics of the polarities in interaction with each other; with a play of yin and yang, masculine and feminine forces, dark and light emotions etc. These polarities interact in a multitude of ways, and strangely, nowhere in nature can there be found a perfectly straight line. The idea of attaining something through a direct linear process is our human creation. It's a curiosity that we have placed great emphasis on striving towards the straight and narrow, when the nature of the process of human development zigzags, cycles and spirals into something new.

Coming to the 4th transition with full commitment will in time awaken an experience that has important consequences for the journey before us. In our human way, we mimic the cycles of nature by using practices or rituals, and repeatedly cycle through these until we reach our threshold for full awakening. Initiations are not always obvious. Sometimes it isn't until we've gone through the build-up and the discharge of old material many times that we pass through the initiation and recognise that we are in a new landscape. Here we recognise the powerful play of the Divine.

Chapter 5

The Heartfelt Revolution

THROUGH A RADICAL AND PERVASIVE CHANGE *in perception with the Dark Night of the Senses we have been sensitized in awareness to the shadow aspects in our life. We have experienced a fall from enchantment where illusions have been shattered. This experience has been an intensely internalized conflict. And though our desire for the light is still strong, we become suspect of anything and anyone that does not match the purity of our vision. We are*

actually living in greater balance with the polarities at this time; yet, it may not feel that way because we have to adapt to the idea of polarities living simultaneously in face to face relationship. We come to see beyond the usual veils that mask us from this perception and begin to take note of discrepancies around us. For example, we may come to view that the community leader, the teacher or person of significance we have been following so devoutly, is not who we thought that person to be. A convergence of conflicting experiences can ensue which generates an active state of rebellion. This is a protective measure; one that may promote a transformation, or lock us into a perpetual pattern of justifying feelings of loss, anger and resentment.

THE REBELLION

This might be called a phase of spiritual adolescence, one that parallels the tensions and pains of the Dark Night of the Senses, but this time the stakes are a little higher. The Dark Night of the Senses brought deeper awareness of self through the discernment of our heart's desire. Now we are challenged to take full ownership of our own process towards its fulfilment. Curiously, through this passage we begin to adjust our role as seeker and follower under the guidance of a teacher or philosophy and begin to touch the integrity of our own authority in our relationship with the Divine. We face an internal power struggle. We are conflicted between the desire to return to the comfort and safety of how things were before or continue with the difficult process that has undeniably altered our reality. This demonstrates how the seeds of awakening are continuously being sown each time we face the question of staying on our comfy chair or taking a step into the unknown. If we are to continue our progress, we have to find the faith to follow our own values. We have a powerful sense that this is how we must proceed, but may not feel quite ready. Again, we come to rely upon our inner compass of intuition.

In order to galvanize a focus of energy and commitment towards greater realization, our frustration and anger at our disillusionment characterize themselves in the form of rebellion.

Our first impulse upon being faced with change, whether small or large, may well be to "put up our dukes" and meet adversity as an adversary. Our instinct is to challenge anything that threatens to alter familiar territory.

The primary objective of our resistance is to protect and sustain us by maintaining our present boundary of awareness. If we investigate the nature of our resistance we will find that it has a logic that mixes emotional and rational elements that together have integrity of their own. This logic is the foundation for the development of behaviour patterns that have become very familiar to us and with which we identify ourselves. We feel safe in this familiarity and like the comfy chair want to stay within it. This creates what we call attachments. Any threat to the integrity of these attachments will cause quite a reaction. If we hold onto these attachments, we will have to reject information that invites us to release from them and change. It requires a good deal of energy to sustain the resistance and hold on.

Our resistance finds the energy it needs by drawing upon the huge resource of power within our instinct to survive. This galvanizes the system into powerful reactions that we can get lost in by inspiring the sense that all we know and are familiar with is going to die if we don't resist the impending changes.

Having found the resistance necessary for our rebellion, we direct it towards people and circumstances that we once emulated and whom we believed represented a certain standard towards the fulfilment. of our vision through their leadership.

We feel lost and upset because the situation is not what we desired or expected. The betrayal we feel is powerful and we want those who have "let us down" to step up, be who they were "supposed" to be and make things right.

The emotional logic of our reaction is quite natural. In response to a need for validation, we blame others and demand that the outside world respond in alignment with our expectations. However natural this response may be, it is actually an adolescent misdirection of responsibility. The pressure to understand and maintain balance in an imperfect and continually shifting world is the cause of great overwhelm. Our energies are dispersed and our identity is in jeopardy. The act of rebellion helps to draw our energies together into a focus.

There are four stages in the process of this rebellion:

» First there is a need to make safe psychological space for personal assessment and assimilation. This is done by declaring boundaries and vigorously maintaining them to establish a protective enclosure.

» Second we begin to distinguish the issues we need to consider by isolating and polarizing them. We attain this by identifying the contrasting elements that caused the disillusionment and separating them enough to clarify our emotional relationship within the situation.

» Third we move into a process of assimilation and realignment. To do this, we recognize how our emotional reactions may contrast with the higher values we've committed to and put us out of alignment with them. Knowing this, we can choose to re-align ourselves and reinforce our personal commitment to the path and values we have chosen. This may be easier said than done. The challenge we face is to recognise that the power of our reactive emotions in the rebellion can be re-focussed. They can be engaged in sustaining and developing our commitment instead of maintaining the static defensive position within the impasse. This step is essential if we are to move forward, for this will open us to the potential hidden within our perceived disillusionment, greatly increasing our self-authorization and give us the vital experience of personal power in transformation.

» And fourth, with the experiential knowledge gained in this process we can reconnect to others with new understanding of the courage required to face ourselves and the skills to create a greater balance of Heart.

The nature of rebellion is a tumultuous and disturbing time. At its foundation it holds great value as it is able to direct us towards a process of individuation. It shows us that we have the ability to hold our ground, define our intentions, focus our actions, and facilitate our own process. In this way we begin to realize that we are stepping forward and becoming the very leader that we previously desired to follow.

A STORY OF RESOLUTION

A middle aged gentleman who was a Rabbi came for a consultation. He had spent the better part of his life offering support to many. He was looking for an outside perspective to help him face heavy duty life changes he was encountering. A few years earlier he had been diagnosed with a terminal illness. He lived in remission for the better part of a year until he received some devastating news: his wife was having an affair with a prominent figure in his community. He was not prepared for this because he felt that his illness, though difficult, had brought him and his wife closer together. What pained him most was the knowledge that many people had long known of the dalliance while he had not. He felt disempowered and betrayed by his wife and his community.

Deeply wounded, he took time away to sift through the wreckage in his heart. Within a short period of time his illness had returned at a considerably advanced stage. Facing a very slim chance of survival he felt outraged. After having labored faithfully so many years as a servant for his faith and community, he had lost his loving connection with God. He was dying and felt completely alone. The emotions of anger and resentment churned within him.

After sharing his story, he stated that what he desired most was to reunite with God and prepare for his passing. Each moment with him felt electrically charged. As we sat there talking, I was intimately aware of this being a life and death crossroad. He was so sincere with his desire. I was curious to see what could change for him, since I knew there was something he would have to let go of in order to fulfill his desire.

As we sat silently, an intense and mysterious atmosphere filled the room. Neither of us knew what was going to happen next; none the less, a deep joy and excitement rose up through my body. He acknowledged that he felt something similar. Looking back, I imagine we looked like two children approaching the playground, eyes wide in anticipation of what lay ahead.

What came of the session was simple and real. He revealed to himself a moment that had been hidden for almost 25 years. This was a key that was to help him understand the importance of the past few years. He remembered sitting at the dining room table telling his family with delight of his decision to become a Rabbi. To his dismay his father rose up from his chair and replied with an abrupt and dismissive statement of disapproval. He was shocked as his father looked him in the eye and clearly said that this was no way of life for his son and without any explanation he left the room.

He was not at all prepared for his father's response and sat frozen. As he recalled this memory, he knew why he had buried it: he couldn't accept how shattered and forsaken he felt by what had happened. Not having his father's blessings caused deep hurt that left him feeling abandoned. He had been unconsciously carrying this hurt and been holding on to so much anger and resentment that he had been suspended in a static defensive position since that time.

Resentment is used as a justification for our anger and hatred. These strong feelings serve to perpetuate distrust. Together they build a wall around the heart to resist life's disappointments and imperfections. This does not mean that these disappointments disappear. The resentment cements a dynamic bond between the resistance and what is being resisted, in this case the disappointment he felt by his father's rejection. This bond can continue as long as we have the energy to sustain it; and becomes a downward spiral that can go on and on.

Now he was able to face and process what his father had said. Through a flood of emotion he released himself from the struggle he was in. He had found the key to support his realignment with his higher values and assimilate the information of the past. This was a major transformation. Through this he was able to reconnect and reclaim his relationship with God. In his words: "I may not be cured, but now I am healed."

STRUCTURES THAT FAIL

Feeling disillusioned and forsaken happens when we are prematurely forced to face the release of something that held a sense of security for us. Being forced to give up something dear shocks us into recognising that there is no guarantee that the world will mirror or provide us with what we think will make us feel safe. The impermanence of our world and ourselves becomes more apparent and we must face any part of us that perpetuates the illusion of permanence. This is an awkward stage for we become transfixed with issues of trust as we are plagued with doubt and questioning everything. It takes a great deal of energy to move beyond our spiritual adolescence into taking responsibility for our growth. If potent enough, the friction we feel from these intense feelings will create the necessary energy to move us beyond the paradox of our delusions and expectations into the next integral part of our journey. Without this friction and the energy it creates, we will remain transfixed in doubt and resentment that others did not live to expectation.

SUSPENSION AND RESENTMENT

Once, as I was attending a Buddhist initiation, the presiding lama offered to tell us his personal story. He wanted to explain a little bit about his relationship with the practice he was about to share with us. The lama described how as a young monk living in Tibet, he was one of a group of monks captured by the Chinese during the invasion in 1959. Unfortunately, as captives, he and the others endured extreme torture over a prolonged period of time. I listened as he described being strung up by rope around his feet from the rafters in the middle of a small room. He hung there for days on end. When the guards were not looking, each of his fellow monks took turns lifting his head so that the blood and pressure could be temporarily released. His fellow practitioners were helpless and felt equally tortured by having to watch their friend suffer so badly.

He explained how this extreme situation catalysed his awakening to faith. He was in such a vulnerable situation that in order to sustain himself he had to find faith. To support this, he consciously chose to invoke his compassion, and chose with every passing day to see his aggressors through his compassionate eyes. His training supported him to remain open in Heart even under extremely dangerous circumstances. Through this, he realized many things: namely that regardless of exterior circumstances he was the master of his soul and creator of the kind and loving space within. He was regarded by his peers as great soul, for even with all the pain and suffering that he endured he could easily make silly jokes and have everyone laugh. His was a truly amazing story of survival and I felt honoured to witness the telling of this intimate journey into love and consciousness. Fortunately, this group of monks were later released and he felt truly blessed to have gained such a deep understanding of his true compassionate essence and had the opportunity to share it with others.

This was the first time I witnessed a Tibetan Lama make use of a personal story as a teaching tool. While listening to his story of courage and faith, we felt the energy of compassion and humanity pervade the room. This energy linked us together and provided the awareness that through adversity we can unlock powerful intrinsic qualities from within. His lesson was that compassionate spiritual practice provided him with a resource to overcome unimaginable suffering. Compassion has an amazingly transcendent capacity and is a primary ingredient for the development of Heart.

The image of this Lama strung by his feet to the rafters later reminded me of an image I had seen many times before: the image found on the twelfth card of the traditional Tarot deck. (The Tarot is set of cards that use archetypical images in a process of divining information.) The image I was reminded of depicts the scene of the hanged man - a person strung up side down by his feet. It represents a passage into a higher consciousness. When our world is turned upside down, we have the opportunity to perceive from a whole new vantage point; everything is suspended as we re-focus to discover the new point of view.

The image on the card shows a person, who though in an apparently dangerous position, is not at all distressed. He is hanging upside down in perfect stillness as if he is in contemplation. The card depicts that eventually we come to realize that struggling is of no use when in a position such as this. Both the Rabbi and the Tibetan Lama had their worlds turned upside down and each had to come face to face with their own mortality. They each came to accept the vulnerability of their situation. This way they found the stillness necessary to realign and reinforce their relationship to the path and values they had chosen.

The way we can tell when we have reached this stillness is when we cease our struggling and release our attachments. Then we are no longer fixated on a specific outcome and open to receive new inspiration. When this happens, we have tapped into a new space that provides for greater understanding of the practical application of faith in our lives.

THROUGH STILLNESS INTO CONTEMPLATION

A loving soul once told me that there is always the possibility of a loving resolution when facing our little deaths. Doesn't matter how many times we have tried, succeeded or failed, each breath is a new beginning. The moment offers opportunity to awaken and open to a free flow of potential with uncommon results.

When tired of struggling by way of our reactions, eventually we understand the futility of strategizing. We come to see that if we want to move beyond our resistance then we must devise a totally new counter strategy. Curiously the new strategy is, in this case, no strategy at all. When we accept and view life from the position of the hanged man, we re-open the gateway for the potential of something totally new to present itself. With the acceptance of all apparent possibilities, we surrender, wait and observe.

To observe without expectation or desired result will induce a quality of awareness that some will call contemplation. Contemplation is really not foreign to anyone. We can slip in and out of it pretty easily. It's a quality of consciousness that has similarities to those moments when we catch ourselves gazing off at a distance. These are fleeting moments with contemplation. We see this with little babies - how they gaze, staring right through us. They have a full presence in pure awareness, but are not conscious of it. If babies can do it, this makes it obvious that contemplation is a natural state that we can fall into with no difficulty. The challenge is to maintain our consciousness within it.

For those who wonder, contemplation is not considered to be the same as meditation for meditation requires that we maintain vigilant focus and awareness. For instance, meditation usually focuses on concentrating the mind on a sound, object or action with the intent of an outcome. The intention could be to calm the body and quiet the mind or it can be to enhance or achieve a higher state of awareness.

So meditation has a function to achieve a goal. The rules of meditation play within our dual reality, whereas contemplation operates without intent; it is relaxed awareness that includes dual reality. Another way to say it is that contemplation is a total state of inclusivity, one that holds nothing outside itself; it, therefore, cannot be sectioned as a meditative state. Contemplation is a graceful state of wholeness, where through simple awareness past, present and future are consolidated. Contemplation has a quality of openness that naturally includes everything.

As adults, our contemplative moments are fleeting and often go unrecognized. It is likely that most of us have lost our sensitivity with it since our early conditioning for survival moves us towards attachment. With practice, we may come to remember this simple way. Through observation and meditation, we can practice and re-sensitize ourselves in a non-distracted and unattached way. The difficulty here is that as soon as we place any importance on the experience of contemplation, it will vanish. For this reason contemplation is difficult to learn and equally challenging to stay with.

To obtain an experience of contemplation, our process requires observation - allowing all impulses, internal and external. It may seem that allowance of this nature would be rather chaotic and, indeed, this is accurate. To maintain grounding in this dynamic situation requires a skilful inner witness who can maintain an anchored relationship in present time reality. If achieved, then, each moment may offer us the possibility of fielding and registering impulses from a clear, conscious and central place of our being.

An original state of stillness may be recovered through contemplation which instinctively helps us to grow by enhancing our acceptance, openness, presence, detachment and inclusivity. It reinstates and develops the possibility of relating to our world from a foundation of inner trust and allows us to respond to it with an attitude of equanimity. It's no wonder then that ancient spiritual texts describe that living in this state without distraction is to be in communion with God, Goddess and all that is.

HEARTFELT REVOLUTION

When it comes to this 5th passage, as mentioned, its' very enticing to become rebellious, resentful and to turn our back from what we were once so attracted to. Any extraordinary experience that has enough power to stop us in our tracks will likely have enough charge to open a few brain synapses, and hence provide a new dimension of awareness. Here the choice is ours, whether we want to use this awakening power for the good of our journey or not. Is our rebellious nature being used in a positive way by defending a cause that will help us progress towards a fuller understanding of Love, or is it motivated by fear and the desire to maintain the status quo? In some way we are faced with an absence of light, an absence of clarity and absence of loving presence; the rebel is inspired into defensive action and tries to convince us that its someone else's fault that everything has gone dark. We are faced with a feeling of being out of control and into the question whether there is such a thing as control. This can become a convincing argument about faith that can lead us into existential angst, and drive us to the question of "whether there is any point in this journey?"

Once long ago, while I travelled with a native elder, we talked about difficult transitions and the bleakness that they can present. Through this discussion the subject of Grace came up as a key element in helping to move through a difficult transition. I said something that caused her to pause. I conveyed through my story an attitude that upset her a little. I recall that I voiced how I had been taught that a person had to earn Grace: only through good deeds and with Divine approval might I know Grace. She turned and faced me with the most loving smile; looking me in the eye, she expressed that without exception all of us are worthy and naturally connected to Grace. She transmitted that in each of us there is a unique impulse towards Divine awareness. This is our personal Grace, and through this impulse the Divine will answer. I was so taken by her statement and by the way she looked at me that I went into a deep stillness for the rest of our ferry voyage together.

In remembering this, I come to see that this impulse towards Divine awareness, this seed of awakening is the impulse that sustains us through these bewildering passages. It is the thread of Divine connection that is with us our entire lives, yet we forget.

In those moments when we are most afraid and closed off from accepting any possibility for change is when we suffer the most. This is when the darkness is most prevalent. When it comes to reorienting ourselves from the loss of an illusion, it may well seem like there are few possibilities. The familiar ground is gone. We are first aware of the bleak darkness of nothingness. But as said before, with the shift from attachment, we may begin to see the possibility for profound transformation. It is a resourcing of the potential we were born with, yet this time with consciousness and intention. Because we've gone through our physical birth, our physiology knows the process of coming from darkness to light. It is our deep somatic sense that can bring this knowledge forward into awareness so that we may perceive the thread of connection with Divine consciousness.

With this perception, the rebellion is transformed into a personal revolution. When we become enticed and excited by knowing there is potential in the darkness and adapt ourselves to take the steps towards our own revelation, we will be realigning ourselves to begin a co-creative relationship with the Divine.

Chapter 6

The Dark Night of the Spirit

THROUGH THIS LAST TRANSITION *we saw the emergence of a potent force, a warrior like quality that holds us up as we learn to stand and face a painful reality. For this next stage, the internal fires continue to burn and transform us, and through this there is now a deep need to be left alone. For some this will be the greatest change of all: to resolve our misgivings through transcendence with the mystical part of our nature.*

As the struggle with our rebellion relaxes we are introduced to an inner stillness that opens the door for a personal revolution to begin. The inner constructs by which we identify ourselves begin to fall apart. Our sense of inner stillness will be continually challenged by the fact that we are losing attachments that we have been using to orient ourselves in the world. The dynamic between our resistance/rebellion to this change and the serene quality in the stillness puts us on the threshold between the panic we feel from our survival system and the possibilities we sense for new connections with Divine consciousness. As we cross this threshold we enter into a truly epic battle and one in which we lose the mind as we know it. On the one hand we feel the potentials of our compassion, our faith, our wisdom and our grace and on the other we are confronted with powerful feelings of fear that are characterized by dispassionate distrust, a strong sense of ineptitude, and a naive helplessness.

This transition is characteristically called the Dark Night of the Spirit. It is a most challenging impasse that is identified by the necessity to let go of all pre-existing systems and signposts we have used to create our identity to this point. This is a passage where we are forced to realize an ability to observe ourselves like never before, and learn the futility of depending on outside sources as a means to secure

*an identity. Our former relationship to the world is
no longer available, and we are overcome by a need
for solitude in order to reflect upon the raging battle
within.*

THE RING OF FIRE

The following is a story of Jean, a colleague, whose journey exemplifies from her tradition the depth of refine-
ment this passage can takes us through. Jean was a
quiet and compassionate person who worked as a
healthcare professional for most of her life. Her gentle disposition and easy going manner allowed her to
enjoy taking life in stride. One of her greatest pleasures
was to meditate daily; she had spent over three decades
perfecting her skills of observation and contemplation
through meditation before this transition of significance
took place...never did she expect that these meditative
skills would play such an important part in securing her
during an arduous voyage through the darkest transition
of her life.

One day during her deep meditation practice she
received an unusual symbol that she identified as Native
American. This was an attractive image that drew her
close to the point where she felt she was being drawn to
move right into the image. Just as she felt herself ready
to merge with this symbol, a fleeting thought came to
her: was it wise that she proceed? Regardless of this
little warning, her impulse to continue was clear and

strong. Jean let go and followed the flow. This decision unleashed a domino effect, as series of internal shifts that would alter her life forever.

From that first image emerged many more. One recurring image was that of a huge black bird on which she felt herself soar through time and space. As she concluded her practice for the day, Jean noted that no matter where she was, new images kept coming. She had a lingering sensation of having tapped into some strange and powerful shamanic reality.

Day and night these intense shamanic images continued to filter into her everyday reality. These moments were now becoming very intrusive for they conjured up powerful, polarising thoughts, feelings and body symptoms. Sometimes these were stark, painful and aggressively dark, while at other times her reality felt wonderfully light, loving, and illuminating. For example she might be sitting quietly having tea when suddenly a sense of anticipation would come over her, a feeling that "something was up". With this feeling of being warned she also noted the recurrence of strong body symptoms like itching, chills, aches, pains or extreme fatigue. All this would be accompanied by the feeling of a dark presence, something that felt insidiously dangerous. When this happened it brought up so much fear inside of her that she could hardly breathe. She would spend hours meditating and praying for guidance and protection, without knowing how or when things would change. Just as the painfully dark passages came and went, so did other passages that were significantly bright and comforting. On many occasions she awoke from a deep sleep with her room filled with a pinkish golden light. Her interpretation was that she was surrounded by an angelic presence for she felt comforted, safe and very joyous. She would sit at the edge of her bed breathing in the sweet aroma and bathing in the lovely glow all around her.

Over the coming months she had lived many truly bizarre distortions, but when she started to talk to "imaginary" people – people nobody else could see, her family became ever more alarmed. Deeply concerned for her sanity and against her will they admitted her to a psyche ward.

This unfortunately made her reality worse. Prescribed medication dulled her out and disoriented her, creating even more distress. Additionally she now felt abandoned by those she trusted and loved. Now weeks later she could say that her future was really bleak.

After going through the process of a deep immersion into the world of psychiatry, doctors and nurses Jean was pleasantly shocked that she was being released from hospital. Despite of all the stressors of the medications and the pervasively strange images still bombarding her, Jean had shown that she was able to maintain strong threads with ordinary reality. She interacted clearly and consciously enough with those who cared for her that she was released...but the process was far from over.

Over the next few years the barrage of strange psychic images, painful somatic experiences and sheer doubt plagued her every day. She began to think this was her fate until one day she faced another transition. Jean describes a marked moment of this long process where she recognised a shift towards a more peaceful and integrated state. On this day she was again taken by this feeling that she was soaring through space on the wings of this giant black bird when suddenly she was catapulted through a tremendous ring of fire. She describes the texture of this fire as being intensely rich in tone, and filled with the colours of the rainbow; rich hues of blue, oranges, yellow, reds and turquoise. As she felt herself pass through this circular opening, the fire completely consumed her and like moving through the eye of a needle Jean felt a shift from her hellish state. From this moment on a gradual and total transformation began to take place. Her thoughts quieted and cleared. Her body pains eased up and later completely disappeared. Her relief was profound; her depth of gratitude sincere. Now she was living from a tender, still and loving space inside. Jean had found her freedom. Her body began to grow healthy again, and it wasn't too long before she was ready to return to her life of service.

DARK NIGHT OF THE SPIRIT

What Jean went through could be described in many ways, most of which were unhelpful to her. Although well intended the mainstream approach was not supporting Jean in all the ways she needed. In her case she was clearly experiencing the passage called the Dark Night of the Spirit. In today's world there is little support in how to manoeuvre through spiritual crisis. What Jean was experiencing may well be a representation of "Baptism by Fire", a time when Spirit is purifying our alignment with Divine intention. This is a time when we are strongly tested in faith, for the outcome is totally uncertain.

That she went through this difficult and dangerous transition on her own is remarkable and it is also the only way it seems to occur. This is a time when we are called to meet ourselves fully. Her volition to maintain clarity and withstand the onslaught of fears and judgement and proceed with meeting each day as best as she could displays a soulful journey that showed the great depths of her true self.

In her book The Interior Castle, Saint Therese of Avila recounts her process with this passage. Her manuscript describes a vision in which there are seven Mansions, each is a passage through which the soul ascends towards union with God. In the sixth Mansion she describes this particular "dark night" with its distinct polarities of dark and light, of yin and yang. She speaks of her process as exceptionally dark, lonely and tormenting, and at the same time filled with moments that are pervasively loving, peaceful and joyful.

Her experience with this passage describes the deepest sense of loss; one of having to abandon, and at the same time feel abandoned by all existing systems that previously organised her perceptions of reality. She speaks of how deeply tormented she felt and how few of her peers could understand anything of her experience. This emphasised a deep sense of loneliness and rejection. What preoccupied much of her thought throughout this bewildering time was to feel forsaken by God, she felt truly alone.

Her close friend and mentor John of the Cross coined the name for this passage. He talks of it as God going after our human nature, exposing our "root" systems to further polish our imperfections, our habits, and our founding attitudes.

Without the restriction of our former ways of interpreting reality, we are left in a space with no distraction for realignment with that which unites in Spirit. In the experience of total darkness we come to know the light and begin to see the possibilities of Union; living beyond the limitations of duality. In that knowledge we can truly feel for those who struggle in pain and darkness. Another level of compassion is awakened for the human condition and all living beings.

With the Dark night of the Spirit, all systems incongruent with this sense of union are being composted leaving a deep sense of emptiness. This offers only one clear option – total surrender into faith and Grace.

AN UNCOMMON DEATH

This transition is first recognised as an experience of extreme loss. In Jean's case her precious loss was the mind that had allowed her to engage in work activity and social life. The process she went through had taken the "normal" out of her life, everyday had become unusually different. As she recounted her story Jean remarked that, previous to this experience, she thought she understood what it meant to surrender. Now she knew that nothing could have prepared her for the depths of surrender she needed to do through with this passage.

This Dark Night of the Spirit is a less common passage than the Dark Night of the Senses for it demands a total redefinition of attitudes and attachments to life's present circumstances. Deep within, this means acquiring an experiential understanding that material reality will not, in and of itself, secure our true identity. When it comes to substantial loss – be it through illness, loss of job or relationship, we face the question of what really is sustaining us. In spiritual matters, great failures and losses may be perceived to strip us bare of ownership, and give us the opportunity to be held by what is eternally present.

This is a big test. With nothing left to hold on to, we must open our eyes to the darkness and come to find the luminosity and nourishment beyond the familiar.

TWO KINDS OF FALLS

There is nothing easy about losing a career, significant relationship, community, or good health. Imagine the pain and disruption if one loses all of these at the same time. The struggle to accept and respect those forces that bring us such devastating experiences may seem totally ridiculous. With big loss comes shock and grief. Shock temporarily secures us and protects from further assault. Grief is a force that intimately acquaints us with the pains of letting go, viscerally engaging the body and mind. Both of these give us full access to our instinctual, survival patterns – the bedrock for the creation of all existing attachments. By shaking this foundation the Divine force means business and presents us with the greatest opportunity for deep awakening.

This big transition can happen to anyone. There is no telling who will go through the experience of it, for it is the soul's journey towards its union with the Divine. Traditionally a spiritual aspirant would have their first experience with detachment through an act of renunciation. In renunciation, a person willingly leaves their common life to live in a temple, monastery, convent, or ashram and gives up all worldly attachments for a life of spiritual service. Not having the distractions of making a living gives time and space for spiritual care. This care can then be offered to the community. Understandably this is a chosen experience and does not compare with the shock of sudden and unexplained losses. The point is:

there comes a time when our next step in our spiritual growth necessitates a total release into faith and Divine awareness. Most often this transition will be accompanied by extreme shift in circumstances. For those living the urban life with everyday challenges there are few structures in place to act as a safety net and to help contextualize this extreme experience of loss and lend spiritual support.

When facing this big passage, the urban aspirant will likely have observed and figured out naturally that time out is essential. There is need for time alone in order to integrate this enforced personal renunciation. At this time we are in such a tender state of being, that our system can only accommodate relationships and situations that are sensitive and understanding of the spiritual process that is occurring. There appears to be a strange veil that acts as a buffer throughout this passage that helps us to filter out what we don't need. In fact it is our extreme sensitivity that acts as our guide. This sensitivity is a double edge sword. It can either overwhelm us to the point of distraction, or act as a representative of our inner wisdom helping to show us the way.

During a personal experience with this process, I had the good fortune of consulting with a kind and wise teacher. She brought to light that her tradition teaches that there are two distinct possibilities when facing a great stage of loss. Here she explained the notion of the unfortunate loss and the fortunate loss.

THE UNFORTUNATE LOSS

Nancy was an ambitious and spirited woman who wanted to make it big with a new marketing business. She was prepared to dedicate all the money, time, and energy needed to build her little empire. Since Nancy was extremely gifted and confident with devising creative ways to support her clients, it was no surprise to her close friends that she achieved great success very quickly.

Within a few years her business had served greater numbers than she could ever have imagined. She had successfully created a lifestyle that gave her ample time for leisure and travel. Within 5 years she had the resources and freedom to hire good people to run her business, which allowed her the privilege of spending even fewer hours in the workplace. With this trend she became increasingly aware that she was distancing herself from work and that her work life had taken a back seat to her social life. Not really understanding why, Nancy knew that she actually preferred to be less involved. Occasionally she would take time to drop in and chat, or have a midday meal with her employees, but seldom did she do more than that.

And then came a sudden economic downturn that took her business through the gauntlet; everything began to fall apart. She was horrified and grief stricken to lay off good employees, people she had come to care for and depend on. Her financial challenges mounted quickly. She had recently purchased a piece of real-estate to accommodate her expanding business and now the abrupt changes where threatening to leave her bankrupt if she didn't find a quick creative way to turn things around.

Most frightening to her was this feeling in her heart that she really wasn't up for the challenge. The fact that she did not want to participate in anything work related still had its hold on her and she couldn't shake it. The shock of the change, the loss of control of her business, and the intense emotion created challenging stressors beyond anything she had ever faced. As her anxiety increased, Nancy felt more and more unstable. With fewer resources at hand to support her, she made some unsound choices. She turned to substance abuse to help her manage the heightened effects of a life out of control. Within a relatively short period of time Nancy sadly lost all she had built.

A loss such as this is truly unfortunate on many levels. In spiritual terms it is only unfortunate if a person cannot learn how to redeem the awareness for growth that the downfall presents. Without strong foundations of faith through which to filter the extreme feelings, thoughts and impulses, the chances of a full recovery are slim. When fame and fortune come about too suddenly and the person doesn't have enough maturity to manage the power of it, like a tower built too high, too fast and without proper foundation; everything can crumble.

Nancy was unable to entertain the subtleties and promptings of what was spiritually possible for her at this time. The shift with her business life was calling her inward to face what the losses represented in her life. She avoided this through the diversion of her social life.

The spiritual lesson during the Dark Night of the Spirit is to transform great loss into something truly meaningful by detaching ourselves from what we perceive we are losing and surrender ourselves to the new possibilities that clear unattached observation may give us. Making discerning choices at a critical time requires that we befriend the unknown, and open to the potential beyond what might seem obvious. If we get lost and distracted by old imprints we risk getting thrown so far off course that we can lose all grounding and sense of self.

THE FORTUNATE LOSS

The outward circumstances of a fortunate loss may look identical to what transpired for Nancy but, unlike her, internally there is an experience of growth and transcendence. Or like what happened with Jean who lost everything, right down to her mind and came out of it feeling that her faith and love for all living beings had grown exponentially.

A fortunate loss means that we come through a tremendous shakedown and recover with increased acceptance and love for the greater Will at play. Even though the passage was deeply painful and we feel we have lost everything; through the process we uncover the seeds for inspirational awakening that bring with it deep feelings of security and joy.

The personal resources that prepare us for managing these extreme moments in life are, in part, due to what belief systems we hold, what tools we have previously developed for self-care, our relationships and the community supports available that help us to face our biggest dragons.

FACING OUR DRAGONS

There is a wonderful story of The Paper Bag Princess by Robert Munsch. It's a tale of reclamation and the journey we must bear to that end. It features a young girl, a princess who has all the riches, as well as the perfect young Prince whom she is set to marry. The story unfolds when a nasty dragon destroys her castle, burns all her clothes and kidnaps her beloved prince.

The princess, a fiery soul, sets off on her journey to meet the dragon and reclaim her beloved. Being stripped of everything, she has nothing to wear and so goes on her search wearing nothing more than a paper bag. Following the dragon's trail, the princess gets lost, but due to her good nature the creatures of the forest assist her to find her way.

Eventually she faces the dragon in his den. Her first attempts to get the dragon's interest fail as she realizes the dragon has no more appetite; he has already eaten his fill for the day. Knowing that her best bet is to use awareness and outwit him, the princess changes her strategy and intelligently recognises his greatest flaws: his arrogance and pride. She decides to stroke his ego by asking him to demonstrate his outstanding powers by performing extraordinary feats. In doing so the dragon completely exhausts himself and to her delight falls asleep.

The princess then enters the dragon's den and finds her beloved. Here in the last twist of the story, the prince sees her and reacts with repulsion because she is wearing only a paper bag. From his reaction, the princess understands that he is not a person of princely character, so she promptly dumps him and continues on her way.

This great little story parallels the journey of this Dark Night in that the young princess is confronted with great loss and stripped of everything. Bearing nothing offers her few distractions and a clear trajectory to the dragon's den. She must go through the deep forest (darkness) with an open heart and find help from the creatures (her wisdom and intuitions). She meets her dragon (imprints of pride, arrogance and greed) and outwits him simply through awareness. She then faces her last obstacle (holding her integrity) and gains true discernment of heart.

The story represents with lightness a perilous journey of consciousness. Do we listen to the dark and agonizing fear of pain and loss, the egos cry for attention, its fury and outrage that things didn't happen according to plan? Or do we possibly stay aware, with calmness while witnessing and honouring the process. Detachment is not about distancing to the point of no feeling, it simply means not taking the common view of reality at face value. It also means having faith that the perception of feeling that all is lost is nothing more than a turning point in the flow towards new potential.

OF THE DIVINITY AND MADNESS

The personal dilemmas encountered during this impasse will push the mind on a new course. In this part of the journey we are losing our mind as we know it. We are being weaned from our previous mental constructs and projections and encouraged to be more contemplative.

The demand to let go of all that is familiar stirs up all our attachments; our beliefs, expectations, compulsions, addictions, our pre-set patterns will flail for attention in their fight for survival. We will feel great fear and distrust. These feelings, once again, signal that a profound transformation is afoot. All our previous experience has been in preparation for this time. Our bid for consciousness and love is being answered with the demand that we let go of all we know and become openly receptive. At this time we don't know what is to come and have to refrain from attaching to speculations.

This can easily place us outside of consensual reality and keeping things together from that perspective may not feel possible. Here is a short story that was told to me by Victoria, a mental health advocate who takes great joy in helping break the stigma that comes with crossing the line into mental illness. Her story speaks of the importance and need for good spiritual care as well as considering the use of allopathic medicines in support of mental and creative balance.

As a woman in her late twenties she incessantly questioned the nature of existence and was continually driven by "Who am I?" and "Why was I put on this earth?" On numerous occasions she felt deeply depressed because nobody could satisfactorily help her answer these questions. Her need to know pushed her to discover and seek until finally she came upon a spiritual path and teachers who could offer her a way to engage her questions and claim her own answers.

Thrilled to have finally found a way to help herself she decided to take even bigger steps. She moved back with her parents so that she could save money and when the time was right she would quit her job and go to India for an extended retreat with a renowned teacher by the name of Papaji.

During the many months of preparation for this big trip, Victoria was delighted to learn that a group of Papaji's disciples were schedule to offer a retreat in her home town. Knowing that this would be the perfect step to help prepare for her big journey, she registered to join Papaji's disciples for a short period of renunciation. Here she would learn how to open herself and be guided into inquiry. All that would be required of her was that she sit on her cushion and observe while she repeatedly asked herself: "Who am I?"

To her dismay her first days of retreat were frustrating and uneventful. Her impatience was getting the better of her, so Victoria decided to push the boundaries a little. She was determined to find real understanding that would tell her that her hours of sitting and listening were not in vain, and so on this particular night she didn't take a break with the other students. She sat comfortably and quietly observed her questioning. And then something of significance did happen. As if a switch had been turned on, she observed that the room took on a hue of sparkle and that her senses were "on fire". Even more amazing was that her sense of self had disappeared. It seemed that all boundaries between herself and others had dissolved.

When other students returned from their meal she felt she could see, feel and hear with incredible depth and this brought great excitement and joy. But something was also a little off. Not only was she acutely sensitive, she also noticed that her interpretation of what she was sensing was a little extreme. For instance, if someone blinked, she would interpret this as much more than just a blink. It could also be an important sign like that of God winking at her.

Her high degree of sensitivity and unusual ways of interpretation stayed with her throughout the rest of the retreat, and though others may have noticed that she was acting a little strange there was no concern brought forward.

When she arrived home, within a short period of time her family noticed behaviours and statements that scared them, and so Victoria was taken to the hospital for psychiatric evaluation. It was then that she was diagnosed with bipolar disorder and with the help of select medications she could reclaim enough grounding and balance to pursue her passionate creative and spiritual life.

In speaking with Victoria of her process she disclosed that one of the most painful aspects of having been diagnosed with a mental disorder was the difficulty in finding proper spiritual care. It seemed that as soon as she crossed that line with the diagnosis, she was being viewed differently than before. She knew in her heart that this process was a spiritual emergency, yet there were few people capable of offering the spiritual care she needed while she continued with her medications. Having a tremendous passion for spiritual growth, Victoria did find a psychiatrist who supported her to look for the care that she needed, but this was not so easy to find.

It had become clear to her that she did have a mental illness as well as being in the midst of a profound spiritual experience. She understood intimately that these were not mutually exclusive and nor did they diminish each other.

It is often difficult for those who have never had the experience of stepping beyond the boundaries of consensual reality to accept the depth and intimate nature of this as a spiritual process. From our cultural perspective there is little value granted to these experiences.

When asking Victoria of the importance and value of her experience, she explained that with this process came many realizations. And these fundamentally changed her way of perceiving life. In her words: "I understood from direct experience that, 'I', did not exist, and that my true self – was pure consciousness that never dies". She had transcended the limitations of mind.

She was then left with the arduous work of integrating her new awareness and balancing it with consensual reality. For this to be achieved medication was a necessary support.

Even though her experience was very challenging, Victoria felt she had been given the answer she had been looking for, not in words but in her whole sense of being.

As spiritual processes go, the dismantling of the mind is an immensely creative and healing time, a necessary gateway for there to be direct knowing and union with Divine will. This is not to imply that all mental disorders are a symptom of Divine activity. What is being said here is that Spiritual emergence pushes for that stronghold of mental control to be released; for only then can full realization set in. As we progress through the different stages of our development the veils or filters that help us to distinguish between internal and external reality get very thin. This is necessary for the establishment of a sense of unity, for that sense of "you and I and the Divine are one". Our Spirit is emerging as an irrepressible vital consciousness. It is cleansing what is obsolete to firmly establish its foundation in the body as our wise and deep self. This only feels like madness. Our job is to understand and know that the de-construction of the mind is because Divine construction is underfoot, and the simplest and most direct approach for self-care is through the practice of observation and contemplation. With this much of the distortions will likely pass as time helps integrate this change.

Divine types of madness have occurred throughout history, perhaps one of the most famous of these is Joan of Arc, a peasant girl who claimed Divine guidance and who led the French Army to several important victories in the fifteenth century. In a culture that carries a great fear of madness, when someone is perceived to be mad or crazy there is a tendency to find ways to modify their behaviour by returning them to the "norm" or marginalizing their presence, "out of sight, out of mind". If they can't be fixed then get them out of sight. Sometimes the "crazy" artist or healer will get away with their eccentric behaviour yet, they already exist on the margin. But for those who live a more mainstream existence there is little room for eccentricity for it may soon be seen as madness. We hide what we perceive does not fit with mainstream perception. This sad misrepresentation reinforces the way we learn how to use denial as a tool to hide from our own fears, and even from ourselves. By accepting this dominant attitude we become complicit in a world that will abuse an individual or a group in order to maintain accepted perceptions of right and sane behaviour. In the case of Joan of Arc she was first perceived and dismissed as insane, then as a heroine, then as a heretic and burned at the stake. As soon as her actions and behaviour became a threat to the powers that controlled the kingdom, she was quickly disposed of. This is but an example of the extreme reaction that can come when the light of God touches powerful systems. This light has the power to penetrate and provide realignment with the values that pre-existed; it is there to help re-establish a unified system of spiritual support. Moving human potential towards higher consciousness doesn't always end up as we would like or hope.

It is important to be aware that during the process of this growth, especially in the passage of the Dark Night of the Spirit, we may face extreme challenges in how the world reacts. In this transformative period we hope to find the Heart and courage to acknowledge and accept the apparent madness. Otherwise the fruit of this change may be lost and the shadows of fear will prevail.

This journey towards self-realization offers all manner of choices. What fits for one person will not necessarily work for another. Yet, it is best at this time to practice deep compassion in a soothing and quieting environment that provides for reflection and self-care. At this stage is the development of an internal relationship to listening. Like no other passage this process cultivates a subtle sense that hones our ability to re-evaluate our relationship to everything. Our intuition and how we make choices are refined, to guide us through the final stages of our dismantling process. In successfully negotiating this stage, we will find independence and no longer be dependent for answers and validation through earthly outside authority.

BEYOND THE MADNESS

I have a close friend who abruptly learned she had stage 4 breast cancer and within a few months the disease progressed to her liver, bones and brain. Within a short period of time she was in palliative care and facing what was apparently inevitable. Throughout her life she had always taken meticulous care of her body. She was a spiritual practitioner of great devotion who had studied at length and had great faith in the spiritual path. When she received the diagnosis all she could say to me was: "How could this happen?" She was in disbelief that she would have to face this dreaded disease. Her first response was to become very angry, and she felt resentment for all those years of fine care she put herself through. At that moment they seemed to have given her nothing.

She was extremely disillusioned, and the treatments for her illness made her so weak, that she had to relinquish all manner of formal practice. She was unable to manage the necessary strength of will to engage in the patterned practices that formally brought her solace. The dissolution taking place was a force beyond her control. She was so challenged that she had to engage every thought, word and action consciously. The cancer engulfed her completely yet she remained in tranquillity, meeting her every moment as quietly as possible. Her life had become a powerfully contemplative journey.

Throughout her process she met with much more than just the loss of her health. She lost her job, her home, both parents and her cherished dog. Her approach to life had to change completely and she cultivated an unusual depth of awareness and compassion. Now five years later, she is in complete remission living a vital life and helping others. She experienced a truly miraculous recovery by doing exactly as was indicated through the flow of events. By allowing herself to be emptied, and by holding to a calm and conscious disposition, she could then allow the light of Grace to take her into a new configuration of life. This guided her towards the manifestation of a new way to serve that would support the light as well as her sensitive nature.

Because she had lost everything and there appeared to be no prospects for her future, she surrendered to the moments she had and became open to receive the new potential that each moment had to offer. Now she saw that those years of self-care and meticulous practice were not in vain. This brought her to develop a level of consciousness in practice that was well beyond her previous experience.

My friend experienced all the elements that are part of the Dark Night of the Spirit in full force; the loss of the mind, letting go of attachments and routine practice, the inability to pray, disengagement from life, the need to be still and tranquil and the overwhelming desire to be with Divine awareness.

The dissolution of all personal structures took her completely out of her familiar rhythm with life. I remember looking into her eyes at a time when it was clear that the illness had the advantage. What I saw was a peaceful woman who had been emptied of all unnecessary trappings, unveiling her quiet, gentle presence.

What force has the capacity to darken and empty the intellect, free the memory and liberate the will? Taking us where we cannot go on our own...

I believe that the Divine force that supports us through our transitions is Grace. Grace could be described like the threads on a great loom providing the main supporting pathways upon which the tapestry of our life may be woven. These primary threads represent universal Grace. It is ever present yet not readily available to our consciousness. The Dark Night of the Spirit loosens the weave of our tapestry enough to bring our consciousness into a closer connection with it and recognise the powerful foundation of Divine intelligence that holds our lives together.

It is truly humbling to be so deeply shaken and come to discover and know that active and ever present forces of a Divine nature are there guiding us. This Dark Night of the Spirit demands that we have faith and surrender to that deep intelligence and be willing to be in awareness and union with a greater presence. Deep experiences of this kind bring an opportunity to cultivate a deeper, more intimate understanding of the relationship between faith and Grace.

Chapter 7

The Invisible Embrace and Self-Realization

THE CHRYSALIS

Through years of spiritual exploration, I have marvelled at how many times the metaphor of the chrysalis and the process of metamorphoses has been used to describe our passage into new forms of realization. Few images equal the perfection of the butterfly emerging from its chrysalis. This complex and beautiful process of deep transformation is a wonderfully appropriate representation of emergence and re-entry into self-realization.

If you watch the process of change, it's fascinating to witness how the transformation begins. It starts with the egg the size of a very small seed. Within this tiny seed are all the necessary elements to produce the butterfly. From the seed emerges the larvae caterpillar who instinctually knows to feed itself as soon as it emerges by eating the leaf it was born on. In the process of its rapid growth, the caterpillar will need to shed its skin several times. When it reaches its maximum growth in its caterpillar body, the caterpillar will move into the third phase of its life process by attaching itself to a leaf to hang upside down. In the beginning this looks like it's just resting, but deep inside there is tumultuous change going on. Here the caterpillar will wrestle its way to shed its outer skin one last time and expose its burgeoning new form, the chrysalis. Within this chrysalis the butterfly develops until it's ready to emerge into its mature form.

There are many wonderful parallels of the butterfly's process with our spiritual development. From the first chapters describing the seed of awareness, the devouring of information to feed the intuitive desire to grow, the shedding of old patterns, the struggle to release ourselves from attachments, all this leads us towards full suspension in the unknown the Dark Night of the Spirit.

Coming through The Dark Night of the Spirit commonly comes with feelings of feebleness and impotency. This is a time when we need to retreat from the world to incubate and integrate our experiences as we move through the last stages of an arduous voyage in consciousness. I cannot imagine a little butterfly doing all its deep inner change without the protection of being securely wrapped in its chrysalis form. Although we do not have the physical form of the chrysalis, our human process at this stage does demand a supportive environment to sustain this period of stillness and introspection.

During this transition, we assimilate and incubate all previous experience into a new body of spiritual consciousness. From the outside all looks still and restrictive, yet on the inside there is much activity. What's going on inside is full of negotiations. Only now we have the awareness of being sustained by Divine Grace which provides a knowing that all is well. This aspect of the incubation time brings with it a delightful sense of the body, soul and spirit being gently kneaded with the most loving and tender hands. It is a blissful and joyful sensation that soothes and engenders a stronger faith.

What may be challenging here is how to maintain the chrysalis-like protective form to give the time necessary to complete the integration process. Traditionally, when a spiritual aspirant was transitioning through this phase they would be in a monastic environment designed to support this development. As urbanites living in the mainstream world, we do not have readily available the luxury of such support and seclusion. As a new life is in the making, we still need to manage our relationship with the outside world. To maintain the degree of awareness necessary to keep this process on track will require diligence, discernment, and devotion to the process. This is an incredible exercise in body consciousness that requires us to be on sensitive alert. At all times we must be listening for the signals that indicate when we have reached our present boundaries of tolerance as well as consistently resonating within the sensations of the transformation itself.

The internal changes occurring will qualify how able we are to respond and manage our relationship with the outside world. We are asked to do double duty by vigilantly monitoring both. Not only must we maintain constant attention on the subtle nature of our internal growth, we must also listen diligently to the signals it gives us in respect to how much outside stimulation we can tolerate. The boundaries we meet here must be respected. Seemingly simple things such as public gatherings, loud events and daily shopping at the market may need to be negotiated in new ways and not just taken for granted. We may also need to accommodate changes for what kind of subject matter we expose ourselves to regarding television, film and world news.

To the outside world we may be perceived as being overly sensitive, yet it is the way it must be. It is essential that during this time we respect the sensitivity as it is our guide for maintaining an atmosphere of compassion for our process. It is not easy to explain our sensitivities and the delicate and sometimes quirky characteristics they present throughout this passage. All this together creates a life circumstance that is definitely challenging for those in the process as well as for family and friends. Compassion and faith overall are the key.

When the time for incubation reaches its conclusion, there is the job of making our way out from our protective shelter into the world once more. This will naturally have a degree of awkwardness, but it will not be as difficult as one may think. Like the ripening of the fruit on the tree, when it reaches it's time it will fall effortlessly to the ground and enter into its next stage of evolution by seeding the growth of a new tree. The balance of timing with awareness in our movement towards integration is an expression of the Divine Grace that guides all stages of our spiritual growth.

The process of shedding our chrysalis is the dissolving of fears, doubts, and unburdening of resentments. Concerns and crisis fade as our process of assimilation begins to kick into high gear. With fewer pending obstacles, integration and realization can accelerate. Our perceptual awareness is shifting, and through the debunking of our personal beliefs and myths, we now have access to a refined sensitivity, an awareness of a new dimension of tenderness.

The quality of this tenderness increases our ability for embodying compassion and opens our receptivity to a brighter edge of consciousness. The experiences of the previous passages were intelligently designed and tailor made to provide the necessary ingredients to unlock our treasure chest and activate our deeply integrated intelligence. The Divine light of consciousness has a mandate to expand and grow. This mandate combined with the drive and energy of our primal instinct gains momentum. This becomes more evident as the Divine light adjusts our primal intention in the direction of a fully unified consciousness.

As we begin our re-entry into the outside world, we meet it with our growing sense of new consciousness. The high degree of sensitivity we have recently been through begins to relax as we acclimatize to the new levels of sensory awareness. What previously seemed unbelievable and insurmountable may not feel quite so formidable anymore. All that cocooned us now falls away and the world begins to take on a whole new tone through an innate joy that seems to come from nowhere. We have gone through a great deal to get here. The transformation required a masterful attitude to allow the awareness of Divine intelligence to unfold from within.

So far, each passage of this book has been describing particular degrees and qualities of dissolution that help lift the subtle veils limiting our understanding of what we can become. Each passage is a cycle of growth with an ebb and flow between the present self and its potential. This is a back and forth movement that gradually moves us within a greater proximity of a more conscious self.

The rocking back and forth can be viewed as the event that awakens our loving nature. Like a good mother cradling us with the fullness of her being, we are guided to awareness that we are being embraced by an invisible force that generously assists us to relinquish the attachments of mind and body. The gift offered is the present moment. This revelation can only come through direct living experience. Each moment, no matter how painful, simple or euphoric the experience may be, holds vital information towards our self-realization and an increased sense of Divine facilitation.

It is like a game of teeter-totter causing interplay of consciousness between heart, mind and body. Little by little we learn to give up the idea that we need to be devoted to one end of the teeter-totter or the other. Now we can allow the continuum of the polarities to co-exist without prejudice. We shift from a constant one pointed focus and move towards seeing life from a broader, more contemplative view. This is a more unified field of awareness that leads us towards increased self-realization and harmony in the flow of consciousness.

A GOLDEN TRIANGLE: THE TRIAD FOR UNIFICATION

The primary ingredient that unifies the relationship among the elements of our heart, body and mind is consciousness. Its growth comes as a result of the intense friction experienced as we work through transitional phases. Like stones being tumbled at the shore line again and again, removing their rough edges and generating smooth surfaces, our transitional phases allow for a more frictionless relationship among the heart, body and mind. The benefit of this transformation of our heart, body and mind is that the essence of each element is more open to receive connection without resistance. Like the polished stones, they are free to experience new dimensions of one and other with an increased intimacy that allows all elements to contribute to a unified purpose. The outcome is a more congruent consciousness that reinforces our awareness of Grace. Through the power of this Grace, each element of the triad between heart, body and mind is transmuted into an exalted aspect of itself. Emotions of the heart are expressed through compassion, the body is filled with a heightened sense of awareness and wisdom of spirit, and the mind is relaxed to move with faith in Grace.

The emotions as the vessel for compassion

Emotionally we have navigated great depths and dis-covered that through our own loving presence we can transform and integrate difficult and sometimes tragic experiences by way of a compassionate Heart. This becomes the cornerstone for how we create equanimity in our disposition with all living beings. As we move towards the experiential understanding that at the source of this compassionate Heart is a love that resides within, we then have more freedom to disengage from our affected ways of relating and move beyond behaviours that are not genuinely com-passionate. With an increased capacity for self-care, we have more affinity for a selfless love and less desire to serve the ego's agendas and manipulations. Having the freedom to love without engaging destructive pat-terns, we may then cease to project our primary needs onto others and can stop playing subtle power games. As a result, our co-dependent roles will dissolve to form a co-creative freedom. Emotional transcend-ence is the compassionate way; a high intelligence that filters all emotion through compassionate eyes – knowing a deep love for all living forms.

The body as the vessel for wisdom of spirit

As we establish our compassionate view, the power of our self-reflection begins to breed greater wis-dom of spirit. This wisdom begins with a deeper understanding that our actions have profound effects and that our body is the vehicle through which we sense and perceive the promptings of Spirit. Through the senses, we are guided towards wise action and into alignment with our primary values. This could be encapsulated in the saying: "do unto others as we would like others to do unto us," commonly known as the golden rule. Self-awareness becomes the perfect antidote to help transform our base of ignorance and deeply seated imprints into discernment and insight. We come to recognise that if our self-reflection is done with compassionate care and openness for change then our comprehensive wisdom of spirit will reveal itself to guide us forward. When we are conscious that this is possible we can transcend the patterns of our intellect and move into the wisdom of our congruent wholeness. This requires an acceptance and respect for the information received through all senses. Through an open and flowing awareness with the body we can know a greater sense of wellness, a wise knowing that is attuned and ready to configure new possibilities: an experience of body as Spirit in the flesh.

The mind as vessel for a greater Will
The adjustment of our primal intention in the direction of a unified consciousness occurs as a result of the awareness that Grace is inherently woven within

the drive and energy of our primal instinct. This is the adjustment of our ability to recognise how the primal will to survive and the Divine Will to evolve in consciousness co-exist.

The primal will's agenda to keep us alive and the Divine Will's agenda to evolve in consciousness remain distinct and feel in contrast to one another until we relinquish enough of the ego's agenda to control everything and release ourselves in total faith. When we accept that primal will and Divine Will are not separate, then we can cease our struggle and enjoy the forces moving us towards wholeness. With time, patience and practice we can give up anger, resentments and fear and be able to create new configurations of experience. Our willingness to practice having faith in the unknown and in relying on Grace as our guide will provide the effect of a unified consciousness with Wisdom and Compassion. These three together - Wisdom, Compassion, and Grace - create a stable triad for the realization of a unified consciousness.

SELF-REALIZATION

The potential for attaining a more unified consciousness resides within all of us. It begins with the subtle seeds for the awakening of the part of us that recognises a curiosity to distinguish and define our unique relationship with the world around us. We create the notion of self through a process of reflecting on the feeling of being simultaneously part of something yet separate from it as well. As mentioned in chapter one, this is the energetic activation of the dynamics between our innate potential and what it needs for its realization of the discerning self. As soon as we have begun to engage in this reflective process of discernment we have begun our self-realization.

Self-realization is often thought of as an end result; a goal we must achieve that is a long way off. Actually the potential for it is with us and available in every moment and we don't have to climb the highest mountain peak to take advantage of it. At any given moment, we are in a relationship with everything and everyone. We may not be aware that we are because it is so obvious that it does not warrant our attention. It's understandable to question what the value would be in considering our relationship to the gas station attendant, the homeless person, the rock star, or the president. Yet, our reflection upon the value of any and all moments of relationship creates a bridge by which we can transcend perceived differences between self and other. It presents opportunities to overcome the judgements of ego that artificially separate us from each other. Even if it's easy to say, getting over ourselves enough to communicate with one another from the standpoint of human equality is not easy. Unfortunately without this, we cannot tolerate the intimacy of relationship that unity demands.

It is curious how the process of self-realization demands an internal investigation of our relationship to the outside world. Our perception of unity changes as we learn to allow the relationship between distinct polarities to exist with each other in a non-defensive way. Through observation, we see that our freedom and self-authorization flourish when we can release attachments that blind us from seeing the humanity before us.

THE INVISIBLE EMBRACE

I remember long ago patiently waiting to participate in a Kirtan. This is a devotional chant that is done in a group, usually through call and response. This evening event was dedicated to help support the victims of a tsunami. The person leading the event was an older and experienced Yogic practitioner. He was a westerner who had spent many years studying in India. To my surprise, this shy reclusive looking man walked up on stage and opened the evening's event with a huge outcry that sounded like a child screaming for its mother. His words were calling for the Goddess Kali and begging her to hear our cries.

Shivers went down my spine as the room went totally quiet. I don't think anyone in that room expected such intensity of sound and power to come from this slender man. We were caught off guard by the sincerity and devotion in his heartfelt outcry. It felt like he was actively reaching out to engage with Kali's divine primordial force of deconstruction, imploring that she be easy on this simple bewildered human race.

His prayers were spoken with humility and servitude and at the same time with a familiarity, as if Kali was the woman next door. His voice rang out through the great hall, and his songs echoed sacred words with incredible clarity and purity of intent. I caught a glimpse of a man who understood how to utilize the engaging power of his emotion, and for that moment we all felt a compassionate embrace within the sounds echoing all around us.

He supplicated himself to these wise and supremely intelligent forces in such a powerful way that it was easy to be moved and taken by the momentum of the chanting. The full power of his love for Kali was palpable and in that moment we were all touched by this realization. I felt the invisible embrace of Grace that comes when the heart is open, and the body and mind are in full response.

Those few hours of chanting had a huge impact on many people. The crowd was deeply moved to dance with tears and laughter. And just like that, as one person touches the graceful web of intelligence wholeheartedly and consciously it affects us all. For this reason, we are all blessed if even just one person has the generosity and care to share the fruit of their spiritual devotion with others. Bearing witness to the realization of another has a soothing effect upon our soul, helps us to maintain the faith necessary to move through difficult times, and motivates our awareness of what great joy there is in serving and easing the pain of others.

Through witnessing the fullness of the Yogi's love and commitment, we all were brought into relationship with each other as well as with our individual mandate for self-realization. We were strongly unified as we shared the resulting relationship from the process of chanting. This was a moment of union that brought tremendous lightness, brightness and clarity of consciousness. Moments like this are instrumental for the creation of a continuous flow in realization.

The more moments we can create that allow us to experience the invisible embrace of grace that unifies heart, body and mind; the more likely we will be able to embody the consciousness necessary for sustained self-realization. Each moment like this that we experience has an energetic resonance that gets stronger and reinforces itself the closer together these moments are. This strengthens our ability to sustain this consciousness and as we do we begin to see that even mundane daily routines offer us insights for increasing our relationship with Divine intention.

DIVINE AFTERGLOW –
REVERENCE AND BEAUTY

Some of the resonance we feel in self-realization comes in the form of awe and wonder. This is what the term reverence means: to be in awe and wonder of that which we are experiencing. We see this naturally in little children. Something captivates them and their faces light up. For that moment, they are full of reverence. This appreciation for life can come to anyone who is awakened to the moment.

This reverence for life is captured through the freshness of the beginner's mind and the openness of a clear Heart. It comes in response to those moments when beauty surpasses its form. The old Yogis outward appearance was not so aesthetically pleasing, yet my perception of him was completely transformed through the love and devotion he exuded. This quality of beauty resonates from an essence within. When this kind of beauty captures us, everything becomes luminous and it is easy to be in reverence.

Through this journey towards self-realization, we become more and more aware of our intrinsic desire to touch and know this particular beauty, that like a magnet, draws us towards our connection with the Divine. Self-realization is a process of coming home to a place of beauty within, a place that lives in harmony with a consciousness that upholds a flowing order.

NEW BODIES OF AWARENESS

The toughest job through this journey is to recognise and celebrate the fact that deprogramming is a natural and regular event in the process of our spiritual maturation.

Each impasse presents an opportunity for transition and growth, and each one asks us to release expectation and attachments that block us from sensing the fullness of our own humanity. It is important to acknowledge that the consciousness of our humanity is the common ground through which we share Divine awareness.

Each stage we have spoken of- The Seed of Awakening, Intellectual Understanding, The Search for Direct Experience, The Dark Night of the Senses, The Heartfelt Revolution, The Dark Night of the Spirit and Self-realization - indicate a shift in consciousness. At the core of each impasse is the same challenge: that of accepting the reciprocal relationship between the polarities of separation and union. As our consciousness grows, we see that they are inseparable partners. We cannot experience one without the other occurring as well. These become the primary themes and polarities through which our spiritual growth will evolve. There are two obvious variations in how these themes are experienced. One requires the process of separation in order to find union, and the other is to find a separate or distinct self through unification.

In the first chapter, Seeds of Awakening, in chapter 5, The Rebellion, and in chapter 6, The Dark Night of the Spirit, the variation on the themes represented is that of separation in order to find union. As an example, the Dark Night of the Spirit demands a strong separation from the world for the incubation of the union with Divine connection. Or in a more subtle way when the Seeds of Awaking stimulate our desire for personal spiritual connection and cause us to separate from our familiar fold in order to fulfil it.

In chapter 2, the Intellectual Understanding, in chapter 3, the Search for Direct Experience, and in chapter 4, Dark Night of the Senses, the theme is of unification in order to find distinctiveness (separation). At first we reach for unification in our understanding through books and the intellectual experience which lead us to a more heartfelt commitment to a path. From there, with the Dark Night of the Senses, begins the process of separating and letting go of obstacles or attachments that limit us from a clear and more loving awareness.

The experience of self-realization is the assimilation of a consciousness that can understand and accept the integration of polarities and has the ability to move between the circumstances of separation and union in a fluid way. Because these themes are so prevalent, we experience the ebb and flow between them at every stage in our development. It is worthwhile to remind ourselves that this is not a linear process. At any stage we may well experience aspects of other stages simultaneously. While we may be experiencing an intense stage of rebellion we may also become aware of new seeds of awareness opening, and calling us to seek out understanding through books or mentorship.

Each stage presents a valuable opportunity for consciousness of our greater potential. Each person experiences this path in their unique way and realizes their potential through whatever form of practice will best suit them. All impasses present us with our unwillingness to expand our spiritual framework. They also provide us with the specific information we need to overcome this resistance and find our way towards Divine unity.

The element that most powerfully assists us in moving through our resistance and into the revelation of our Divine connection is Love. Love is the umbrella under which all aspects of Heart unify and it provides us with a consciousness that continually refines itself into a tenderness capable of transforming any impasse into a passage way. Love is the unifier. The impasse is the divider. In the spiritual process, we will always encounter both, and need to accept both to realize our potential for Divine connection.

Chapter 8

Security During a Strong Transition

THE ELEMENT THAT MOST POWERFULLY assists us in moving through our resistance and into the revelation of our Divine connection is compassion. Compassion is the umbrella under which all aspects of Heart unify and it provides us with a consciousness that continually refines itself into a tenderness capable of transforming any impasse into a passage way. Compassion is the greatest unifier.

When it comes to the sensitive issue of relationship and community there can be two strong tendencies.

Sometimes the process opens a recipient and existing relationships to a direct experience of love, as the opening of one person's heart can trigger a similar effect for those in close relationship. The warmth and joy of sharing this love awakens a heartfelt connection that is very strong and very special.

And then there is the possibility of difficulties arising in relationship. Here is the need for all to look at the issues of compassionate relating. This is important to look at because relationships are the spider's web, they are the threads that allow for connectivity and exchange of consciousness, and they are the pathways that foster growth during vulnerable moments. When someone goes through a deep recapitulation of their life, their process and the reconfigurations they come to, will naturally touch all pre-existing relationships. This is not always easy for those who do not have the depth of experience and understanding for such an exchange.

For the spiritual practitioner, the difficulties that surface at this time are likely exposing deep roots of issues, patterns of relating that were established long ago, and most probably in early childhood. How relationships unfold, how we relate to one and other, friends, to family, and community or spiritual group will open the door for creating the necessary shift towards a new personal as well as collective order.

It's inevitable since the greater the transition, the greater the shake up and sense of disorientation with life therefore the deeper the need will be for a strong collective to help sustain faith and relationship with God. If a person goes through a strong transition that causes excessive stress or possibly trauma, the combination of emotional, mental, spiritual and potentially social challenges increases. The shake-up exposes the need for clarity, but also the need for all to unlearn what we were exposed to that can hinder healthy reclamation. This also exposes the deepest of vulnerabilities we have as humans. This exposes the need for security, for compassionate embrace, and to feel safe and protected so that we can rest in the light of kindness and reconfigure with the change that is underway.

What helps in attaining enough security to withstand the high degree of change is to be able to turn towards a spiritual family or group and make a plea or request for refuge. The outcome of this will affect how everyone moves through the transition, meaning how the group relates to the one going through the impasse and how the person who is suffering relates to the group will influence the outcome. The responsibility for this lies not only in the hands of the one undergoing the transformation, but importantly with the spiritual group and its leaders.

When it comes to the letting go of a deeply rooted foundation pattern, what secures and fulfills us is to know that in the physical world we are sustained by the loving energy of community and friendship. Without this the outcome for a healthy transition can feel completely daunting and overwhelming, for without compassionate support the prospect for positive outcome is greatly diminished.

When going through the later transitions, as mentioned the spiritual practitioner is moved to let go of outward responsibility like work and other outward commitments. To do this and be left without the positive influence of a social container leaves the person disengaged from the powerful threads of community that stabilize. This is to realize that the momentum of a strong impasse can require that the individual take considerable time out to rest and contemplate the deep change, and that the positive influence of a respectful compassionate communal presence supports the transformation underway. It encourages new growth, new depth in relationship and greater sustainability for everyone.

What I speak of here is extreme, and not common. But it does happen that for certain individuals going through an impasse, they may be called to make a most powerful act of faith and approach those who may not have the personal experience or understanding of what is truly transpiring. The approach is a plea, a request for mercy, a request for refuge, to be compassionately held.

To make this request for refuge exposes such a deep level of vulnerability, the risk is great yet if properly expressed and received, the potential outcome will foster tremendous healing for all involved. As in the Buddhist philosophy the Sangha or group has the potential to offer a powerful grounding which can really help to reorient and establish a sound foundation, one that is in right relationship to spiritual values. If this container does not get created during the more refined and sensitive passages; there is a tendency towards greater loss for all and a lack of consciousness that will foster a lack of compassionate sustenance in the community. The loss of communal relationship creates a penetrating wound so deep, that the reclamation of heart may never then be fully fulfilled.

It is my prayer, that should you be in the midst of a challenging impasse, that you be provided with the love and tenderness of likeminded people. May your spiritual journey be blessed with the loving presence of friendship and community.

Chapter 9

Tools for the Path

THROUGHOUT THIS BOOK I MAKE REFERENCE
*to doing practices as a way to develop awareness
and gain knowledge of ourselves. Regular practice
is an important part in the process of our spiritual
development. We need practical tools to help us
stay on course and build the special kind of muscle
required for the sensitive journey ahead. As I draw
this book to a close, I want to offer a few simple, safe
and timeless techniques to help sharpen awareness,*

reduce stress and ease conflict through any level of transition.

MINDING OUR OWN BUSINESS

In the beginning chapters I spoke of imprints: those habitual patterns that cause us to create the same outcome time and time again. Though sometimes conscious, these are mostly unconscious thoughts, words and actions. Some of these imprints will be positive, and some will be negative for they can lead us in the opposite direction to what we desire. When we were young, we had little power to affect our life experiences or the imprints they created. As adults we now understand that unless we alter some of these we will be repeating the same old patterns and have less influence in the course of our development.

Here is a strange little story to help understand the power of an imprint and how easy it is for a senseless or unwelcome habit to go unnoticed. The origin of this story is not clear, since I have heard it told in a few different ways. It's the story of a curious cat, a spiritual teacher and his disciples.

One day during the evening practice a cat ventured into the meditation hall and began to distract the students from their work. The teacher requested that the cat be taken outside. Unfortunately, the cat kept finding its way back into the room. The teacher then had the cat taken outside and tied to a banyen tree. The cat, annoyed but not hurt, survived this ordeal and later was released when evening practice concluded. The next day the same thing happened. The cat found its way into the meditation hall and was again tied to the tree. After repeating this over the course of a few weeks, it became part of the evening ritual for students to run around looking for the cat and tie it up before evening practice. Over the next few years everyone had forgotten how this all began. New students never questioned the significance of this evening ritual and the old teacher who started this had left.

In time the cat dies and there is sadness for the loss of the creature, yet there is also concern about finding another cat to tie up to the banyen tree before evening meditation. And so students go off to town to find another cat. Centuries later when descendant students of the spiritual teaching are questioned on the significance of tying up a cat before spiritual practice, all manner of elaborate explanation came forth, when the real answer was so that the cat wouldn't bother them during practice.

In the telling of this story the imprint was set up at the teachers request to tie the cat to the tree. It came about first with a thought, then a few words and lastly through the teachers clear action. With the repetition of this sequence an imprint was born and the power of its continued effect lingered long after its practical purpose was remembered.

Many imprints are created throughout our life. Some will be helpful to us and some will hold us back. The trick is to find the ones that don't serve us any longer and change them. How we come to recognize and change those imprints that block us from our development requires some conscious steps.

#1 – OBSERVE

The word observe translates from its Latin roots ob =over and serve =service or watch to mean serving over or watching over. To watch over the ways we speak, act and think is a necessary skill to develop if we want to gain awareness for growth and change.

Observation as a practice can be engaged in anywhere and anytime. Through observation, we view individuals, situations, activities from a neutral perspective. It is sometimes described as the choiceless witness since we attempt to remain somewhat neutral towards what we are looking at. Like a camera lens which has no judgement, observation amounts to "just taking the picture." When we observe, we open the lens of our awareness to help get a better glimpse of the whole situation. In this way we experience our thoughts, feelings and actions without getting swept away in them.

Observation is a great skill to learn for it helps ease our tendency for attachment and allows us to be more open minded. As we remain aware within the state of observation, strong experiences will be less overwhelming because we are able to step back a little to appreciate the natural flow of events. I like to think of observation as a good inner parent who offers us the qualities of kindness, patience and perspective yet allows the experience to happen without interpretation. Developing our observation skill can come quite naturally with only a few minutes of daily application. Here are a few simple and easy ways to bring this practice into daily life:

1 – This first exercise is done for a few minutes at a time in a quiet place. Sitting comfortably, begin by noticing how it feels to have your body supported by the chair beneath you with your feet firmly connected to the ground below. Relax into this awareness and take note of the skin layer surrounding your body. Consider how it is a natural boundary between you and the space around you. While you are sensing this space around you and the ground beneath you, begin to focus your attention on the flow of breath within you. Take some moments to feel the movement of your breath. Sense the air flowing gently in and out of your nostrils. See how long you can hold your awareness of these details mentioned simultaneously.

Although this exercise is fundamentally simple it is also the foundation for advanced practice.

2 – Another simple exercise is called gazing. This can be done pretty much anytime, but it's really lovely when done on a beautiful sunny day, or later at night. To begin, sit or lay down to make yourself completely

comfortable. If done during the day, bring your attention to the dappled sunlight filtering through the leaves
of a tree. With eyes semi-opened let the play of light and
colour wash over you and take note of subtle changes
as your senses are stimulated. This is a delightful way to
relax and appreciate natural beauty.

If done at night, look up to the night sky and gaze at
the moon and the stars. Both of these gazing exercises
are simple yet effective ways to quiet the mind and take
in the bigger picture.

3 – One ancient Hindu technique for developing
keen observation skills is called tratak or fixed gazing.
It involves concentrating on a single point or candle
flame.

To do it, simply sit in front of a lit candle (beeswax
preferred). The flame should be at eye level, about three
feet away. With slow, gentle breathing, gaze stead-
ily at the flame without letting yourself be distracted.
If thoughts arise, simply let them pass by. Consistently
bring your attention to the flame before you. Try to keep
your eye lids open and not blink.

Imagine the flame is entering your body through
your eyes and illuminating your inner being. Continue
this activity for a few minutes or until your eyes begin to
water. Gently let the eyes close and observe the image of
the flame in your mind's eye until it disappears.

At first your eyes will want to blink and there might
be a slight feeling of discomfort. Yet, with practice, you

will be able to keep your eyes open and this will make it easier to see the flame when you close your eyes.

To finish you may wash your eyes with cool flax or rose water to end this practice with a soothing, cooling and comforting sensation. This ancient practice helps to open the 3rd eye and strengthen the skill of observation. It is best done with a pure beeswax candle since there are fewer toxins released and the flame of the candle is softer and gentler than petroleum or paraffin based candles.

#2 – CLEAR IMPRINTS

One evening over a cup of tea, a fellow practitioner confided that she was looking for a new relationship. She had been living on her own for almost 10 years and had never married. Having reached midlife, she could not imagine living the rest of her life without companionship and declared that now was the time for her to take charge and "find herself a man."

She was ready to take on the task of changing her deeply seeded pattern of living independently. She was prepared to do the detective work required to spot those thoughts, words and actions that did not match up with her vision for a loving companion. She would need to track herself and watch for the subtle ways that her thoughts, words and action might be contrary to what she was asking to receive in her life. By doing this, she could become conscious of any mixed messaging and in doing so stood a good chance of making a leap towards real change.

As in the earlier example of the cat and the banyen tree, our imprints develop from logic that at one time made sense to us. As we repeat these patterns time and time again, they can lose their relevance to present time needs and could actually hold us back from our desired goals. Usually we don't have much awareness of the subtleties that support our imprints, or if we do, we feel helpless in the face of them. Our subtle thoughts and feelings forecast our future by projecting themselves subconsciously into present time. These projections are really our defence mechanisms, our ways of protecting ourselves from the unknown or from a potentially painful reality. They sit at the foundation of our actions and will not change unless we open the window of awareness for new consciousness to breeze in.

To become aware and change our imprints and their projections will require keen awareness on our part. The thoughts, words and actions that flow from our imprints are powerful pathways for manifesting both what we want and don't want.

Once we decide to change an imprint, we must recognise what elements we are acting on that do not match up with our vision. The stronger the imprint, the stronger will be the projections that work to keep things as they have always been. The older the imprint, the stronger the projection will be and the greater the probability of discovering that some part of us does not want to know of any other possibility. This is what we want to watch out for.

For instance, my friend noticed that when she started to set up date nights, all kinds of negative thoughts flooded in. She was recalling negative statements she had been repeating for years. The sad thing was it discouraged her to hear herself say these things. It left her feeling like nothing would ever change.

Our imprints are like boxcars of a train: they come as a chain of thoughts, words and actions which are interdependent of each other. If the imprint is like a series of boxes and the projection is the glue that holds it together, then the most direct way to reconfigure the imprint is to disengage the chain that secures their interdependence. We begin this by recognising any boxcar of the chain we are in - and begin to project our thoughts outside of it. In other words, by the simple act of choosing to look outside the box and consider other possibilities we can make huge changes in our life. This is like sending a fishing line of faith outside the box into the infinite potential beyond. The action of considering that possible alternatives exist even if we don't know what they are at the moment begins to dissolve the projections that hold the imprint together.

If my girlfriend begins dating with the underlying perception that there are no good men available, the outcome will be clearly negative. If she consistently tracks herself to become aware of underlying perceptions that will likely prevent her from achieving her vision, spots a defeating statement and poses the question: Now what is beyond this thought? She sends out her fishing line into the infinite potential and opens her mind to the possibility of an alternative outcome.

Life gives us all kinds of opportunities to untangle ourselves from old imprints. If we take the time to recognise that this is a game of projections and that we can become the master of the projecting system then it's a matter of spotting when we hit the replay button.

It's to be expected that our old imprints and our present desire for a different outcome will come into battle and possibly create an impasse. To move through this requires that we suspend our thoughts, gestures and actions, even if just momentarily, in order to observe our boxed in thoughts and move beyond them.

When it comes to fulfilling our need for love, compassion, wisdom and grace it seems obvious that the actions required will be those that have these very qualities we wish to receive. Meaning, if we are looking for generosity then we do well to give generously to self and other. The actions we take powerfully effect and stabilize our desire for change. So, if we want a different outcome we must choose different actions.

An example of this was a colleague who was going through a horrendous Dark Night and found ways to identify and take action to change the painful imprints she was working with. She was a physical therapist in her mid-forties who was shocked to find out that she needed a hip replacement. She was facing the obvious physical challenges of her situation as well as the possibility of losing her career.

Having been a spiritual practitioner for many years, she came up with a simple strategy that would help her open to infinite possibilities. She understood that if her fears had their way, her life would be a disaster. She also understood that her actions were an important gateway through which she could direct herself towards the change she desired to see.

As she went through her morning practice, she set up two lists. One was a list of names of people who she knew were suffering and needed support. The other was a list of those caregivers who would support her through her transition. These were friends, family members and professional caregivers she would be depending on through her healing process.

At the end of her morning practice, she would dedicate the merit of her spiritual work for that day to each of those on the lists. She felt that this action of giving would help to change the pattern she had of perceiving herself as isolated and without the necessary resources to pull her through the difficulties ahead. This was the action of giving to others as she would like others to give unto her. The outcome of this action resulted in a tremendous outpouring of support from her community in all levels of her life.

PRARTHANA

I will never forget one of my first teachers, a Native American elder who upon our first visit together opened our session with a prayer that was so sensitive and engaging. She encircled my body while waving her abalone shell, the threads of spiralling sage smoke filled the room leaving a lasting impression upon my senses. This moment held great significance for me. It helped me cleanse a deeply held resistance to prayer practice for this was my introduction to spontaneous prayer of a loving nature.

For the first time I was to experience a depth of contact, a tone and sincerity of heart that instantly relaxed me. I was so moved by the quality of presence she invoked that I was able to let go and touch a real spiritual need. Through this preliminary teaching, her guiding message was that prayer is a simple and profound healing tool as well as a common way to magnetise the right people and healing conditions into our life.

The word prayer is derived from the Sanskrit word prarthana = prar + than = meaning to make a passionate plea. Prayer as a simple spiritual practice has stood the test of time. Throughout millenniums it has been the back bone of spiritual and religious traditions, and to this day it exists as a foundational form of practice for the novice as well as the adept. It works on the principles of mixing the frequencies of the human voice with heart-felt passion. This is a principle that creates magnetism and allows for Divine forces to assist by measure of our receptivity. To whom we pray is of personal choice.

Prayer is a direct action, a step that anyone can use to attract what they need to help avoid and transcend obstacles. In many cases people don't know that prayer as a tool comes with stages of progression. These stages when understood can deeply influence our spiritual development, not to mention that when the going gets tough it is usually a foundation of practice to fall back on.

With spontaneous prayer there are opportunities to express, listen and learn. To be effective with prayer, it helps to understand the simple steps that help to manifest the guidance we seek. Here are four stages briefly explained.

Stage 1. – Express what you feel. Expressing starts with a sincere statement of how things are. This concerns our present circumstances, a time to say things from the heart without fear of judgement. Here we offer ourselves a little therapy session and allow for self-witnessing and the welcoming link with Divine forces. So speak as though you mean it, for emotion ignites passion - the fuel for relating at all levels. Sometimes the act of praying will bring up unfinished business. This is a time to welcome the opportunity to discharge excess emotion and mental fixations.

Stage 2. – Declare what you need. When you have finished expressing what you feel, it is then time to take a moment and reflect on what might be needed to help transcend our obstacles. Perhaps the need is for direction and proper guidance, or perhaps we haven't a clue of what we need. All this can be expressed. Getting clarity for our personal needs and learning to express them helps us accept our vulnerability.

Our vulnerability holds both the potential to react in defence and reinforce our attachments as well as having an element of openness that prepares us to be able to receive new information. We face this crossroads whenever we encounter the unknown. Do we choose closure, or openness?

Here is a short dream sequence that describes how openness, clarity and intent can guide us.

The dream begins with a scene where a woman is in a car with friends. They are moving at high speed down the highway, the general tone is quiet. Unexpectedly the car comes to a stop, and the woman is dropped off. At first she thinks she is to look for a washroom, but then she realizes she is literally at a crossroad, with four roads leading to nowhere visible – and she is totally alone for the car has vanished. The only structure around is a wooden bus shelter with its awning above her. She stands there feeling perplexed with no idea where she is or where she is going. With a moment's pause she realizes to pray and ask for help about what to do next. With this thought, her dream opens up and before her is an older gentleman offering her his cell phone. The woman makes a call for help and then wakes up from the dream.

Stage 3 – Sense your gratitude. Now that we've made our statements and expressed our needs we end with a statement of gratitude. Anything we feel we can honestly be thankful for including the opportunity to pray will assist us to appreciate that there is goodness in our life. This will help us to gain confidence with issues of uncertainty and also strengthen the bridge with those benevolent forces that we are reaching to relate with. Gratitude helps to further open the heart and by counting our blessings sets us up for greater receptivity.

Stage 4 – Listen with the body. This is the resonant part of prayer. We have expressed our feelings, our needs, our gratitude, and now it is time to be quiet and listen. Listening allows for reflection. Watch for the signals that lead to an understanding of how interconnected everything is. Through this process, we witness the bigger picture and more accurately perceive our relationship with the Divine.

Together these four stages of prayer are a strong practice and will contribute greatly in assisting us in times of need.

PREPARING THE VESSEL – THE BODY

Our body's tissues are sensitive and intelligent. They resonate to subtle changes of mind, emotion and spiritual influence. This prompts the movement and cleansing of debris through subtle energetic pathways. Some of these pathways are familiar to us as acupuncture channels. With correct training and under the right conditions, these subtle pathways can be opened, strengthened and supported to help us create greater vitality, mental clarity and ease for our development.

As we go through our metamorphosis and engage in this incredible potential for change, it is important that we take care of our physical health. If we support the body as it adapts and transforms itself into the vessel for greater consciousness, we can prevent illness and obstacles on the journey.

A classic and true account to this effect is the story of the wandering Hindu Prince Damo, a Buddhist Monk who for a brief period of time served Emperor Wu of the Liang Dynasty. Before too long he fell out of favour with the emperor and found himself wandering north towards the Shaolin temple.

At the time of his arrival at the Shaolin temple, Damo was not well received. He spent upwards to 9 years meditating and contemplating in a nearby cave. Throughout this time, he carefully observed the movements of animals which brought him to develop a foundation for health protocols that would later be known as Chi Kung.

During Damo's time in the cave, a monk from the Shaolin temple by the name of ZhiRen fed Damo daily and was deeply influenced by the spiritual eccentric. It was through ZhiRen that Damo's new knowledge for health protocols was shared and in time Damo was invited to join their monastic life and help the ailing Shaolin monks. He taught them how to heal their physical ailments by cleansing and developing the energetic pathways of the body. This not only brought greater health, but also assisted them in their spiritual growth by supporting the energetic pathways of the body to hold greater amounts of energy and consciousness. The principle of his teaching was sound: as we develop and grow spiritually our body also needs to be supported.

In our spiritual process, the subtle channels in the body will continuously be purified with greater charges of light and consciousness. As we become accustomed to these higher levels of light and consciousness our channels will flow with a wisdom that is relative to the degree of our awakening. Because the body is the vessel for this wisdom it needs special care and maintenance.

We have available many systems of knowledge that offer practical support to secure the body as it goes through its transformational process. The sophisticated system of knowledge that Damo developed is called Chi Kung, which literally translates as energy management. With over four thousand different forms of Chi Kung now being practiced, it is obvious there is much to choose from today. It is wise to include Chi Kung in daily practice, for Chi Kung calls us to consider the whole body as the instrument for our spiritual evolution, the anchor and pool from which all experience will flow.

As I conclude here are few final thoughts for the path ahead:

- » Maintain your health – don't give more than you have.
- » Pay attention - practice observation.
- » Set priorities – continually observe your values.
- » Be honest with yourself.
- » Acknowledge the shadow – be careful of overindulgence.
- » Be clear with your motivation - take action wholeheartedly.
- » Do no harm, respect all other members.
- » Take it one step at a time.
- » Don't take things so seriously, laugh and enjoy the process.

Notes:

Thank you for reading this collection of stories and teachings. The purpose for this writing was intended to share some frameworks and experiences that might assist in moving through some of life's difficult passages and relating them to the process of spiritual development. The stories and individuals I have written about are creative compilations that draw together events and experiences from many different people and sources I have encountered over the years.

    I would like to dedicate the merit of this work to all those who meet difficult passages in the process of their spiritual development. May your journey be blessed with compassion and guided by Grace.

About the author:

Denise Richard brings the knowledge and understanding of many years of study as a multi-faith spiritual practionner. She has enjoyed her investigation of practice in Buddhism, Hinduism, Taoism, Shamanism, Christianity, Tai Chi and Chi Kung and brings this unique understanding in how this knowledge can be applied for unveiling and healing the Heart. Her passion for spiritual studies combined with her direct experience has given her a profound understanding for how realize spiritual potential in day to day life.

For further information about upcoming courses and sessions contact:
firesofcompassion@gmail.com
www.firesofcompassion.com

Bibliography

Alstad Diana and Kramer Joel. The Guru Papers. Frog Ltd.
    1993

Chodron, Pema. When things fall apart. Shambala
    Publications, 2000

De Leon, Carlos, Atrevete a ser libre (Dare to be free)
    Edamex, 1989

Grof, Stanislav and Christina. Spiritual emergency.
    Thatcher/Putnam, 1989

Levine, Peter. Waking the Tiger. North Atlantic Books,
    1997

McNally Christy and Roach Michael. The Diamond Cutter.
    Crown Publishing, 2009

McNally Christy, Roach Michael and Gordon Michael, Karmic Management. Doubleday, 2009

May, Gerald. The Dark Night of the Soul. Harper Collins Publishers, 2003

Moore, Thomas. Care of the Soul. Harper Collins Publishers, 1992

Moore, Thomas. Dark Nights of the Soul. Gotham Books, 2005

Ray, Reginald. Touching Enlightenment. Sounds true publishing. 2008

Rinpoche Namgyal. The Womb, Karma and Transcendence. Bohdi Publishing, 1996

St. John of the Cross. Dark Night of the Soul. Dover Publications, 2003

St. Teresa of Avila. Interior Castle. Dover Publications, 1946

Trungpa, Chogyam. Cutting Through Spiritual Materialism. Shambala Publications, 2002